222 Easy Italian Recipes

WHITE STAR PUBLISHERS

GRAPHIC DESIGN BY **MARIA CUCCHI**

WS White Star Publishers® is a registered trademark
property of Edizioni White Star s.r.l.

© 2010 Edizioni White Star s.r.l.
Via Candido Sassone, 24
13100 Vercelli, Italy
www.whitestar.it

Translation: Catherine Howard

ISBN 978-88-544-0557-8
1 2 3 4 5 6   14 13 12 11 10

Printed in China

EDITED BY

★ ★ ★ ★ ★

ACADEMIA BARILLA

PREFACE BY **MICHAEL WHITE**

CONTENTS

Endless Possibilities

by Michael White

My LOVE FOR ITALIAN FOOD, PARTICULARLY FROM THE EMILIA ROMAGNA REGION, WHERE I TRAINED FOR MANY YEARS, IS GROUNDED IN THE ROOTS OF THE ARRAY OF FRESH PRODUCTS AND IN-GREDIENTS THAT ALLOW MY MIND TO RUN FREE AND DREAM OF ALL THE POSSIBILITIES FOR CREATION AND INNOVATION. ALTHOUGH THE CORE FOUNDATION IS TRADITIONAL AND FALLS WITHIN A "PERIME-TER" OF WHAT TRULY CONSTITUTES AUTHENTIC ITALIAN CUISINE, THE DEPTH AND BREADTH OF THE IN-DIGENOUS PRODUCTS PROVIDES SUCH A STRONG CHANNEL FOR NEW COMBINATIONS AND NEW EX-PERIENCES FOR ME THAT TODAY I FEEL LIKE THE FIRST DAY OF MY EARLY APPRENTICESHIP IN IMOLA. SIMPLICITY IS THE HALLMARK OF ITALIAN CUISINE. IT WAS IN ITALY WHERE I LEARNED TO APPRECIATE THE SPLENDOR OF INGREDIENTS FIRST HAND. THEREFORE, WHEN LOOKING FOR NEW INSPIRATION, I LOOK NO FURTHER THAN THE "CUCINA DELLA NONNA," (GRANDMOTHER'S COOKING), "CUCINA POVERA" (HUMBLE DISHES), "CUCINA RUSTICA" (FARMHOUSE COOKERY). MY PASSION FOR PASTA AND ALL THINGS ITALIAN EXTENDS FROM THE SIMPLEST OF INGREDIENTS SUCH AS THE AGEING BEAUTY OF PARMESAN CHEESE, PROSCIUTTO AND BALSAMIC VINEGAR TO THE MOST HIGHLY REGARDED WHITE TRUFFLES AND BAROLO.

THE NAME BARILLA IS SYNONYMOUS WITH THE WORDS QUALITY AND CONSISTENCY. LIKE BARILLA, I STRIVE FOR PERSONAL EXCELLENCE AND CONTINUOUS INNOVATION IN MY CRAFT. I INVITE YOU TO TAKE THIS JOURNEY WITH ME TO DISCOVER THE ENDLESS POSSIBILITIES OFFERED BY ITALIAN CUISINE.

ACADEMIA BARILLA

A Worldwide Ambassador of Italian Cuisine

Parma and the surrounding area boast some of the most famous local typical products in the world, such as the famous cold cuts, cheese and pasta. This city, which has an ancient tradition in food and agriculture and which is recognized worldwide as one of the most prestigious capitals of cuisine, has witnessed the development of the Barilla Center, designed by Renzo Piano; a modern building that houses the Barilla Academy (Academia Barilla). Academia Barilla was founded in 2004 with a mission to assert the role of the Italian art of cooking, to protect the Italian regional gastronomic heritage by safeguarding it against imitations and counterfeit products, and to appraise the notable Italian restaurant tradition through significant investments and dedicated events. It is a meeting place for outstanding professionalism and unique skills in the world of cuisine. The institution organizes courses for cuisine enthusiasts, offering dedicated services to operators in the cuisine sector and promoting very high quality products which are the result of age old knowledge.

ACADEMIA BARILLA WAS AWARDED THE 2007 "PREMIO IMPRESA CULTURA" (THE COMPANY CULTURE PRIZE), FOR ITS EFFORTS IN PROMOTING THE CULTURE OF ITALIAN CUISINE AND CREATIVITY ALL OVER THE WORLD.

THE PREMISES WERE CONCEIVED TO ADDRESS THE SPECIFIC REQUIREMENTS OF TRAINING IN THE FIELD OF FOOD AND COOKING AND ARE EQUIPPED WITH ALL THE MULTIMEDIA TOOLS THAT ARE NECESSARY TO HOST BIG EVENTS: AN EXTRAORDINARY GASTRONOMIC AUDITORIUM IS SURROUNDED BY AN INTERNAL RESTAURANT, A POLY-SENSORIAL LAB AND VARIOUS LECTURE ROOMS, EQUIPPED WITH THE LATEST TECHNOLOGY DEDICATED TO THEORETICAL AND PRACTICAL TRAINING. IN THE GASTRONOMIC LIBRARY THERE ARE MORE THAN 9000 VOLUMES ON THE SUBJECT AS WELL AS AN UNUSUAL COLLECTION OF HISTORICAL MENUS AND PRINTS ON THE ART OF COOKING. HERE, PROTECTING TRADITION IS COUPLED WITH INNOVATION, THANKS TO THE USE OF INNOVATIVE COMMUNICATIONS TOOLS: INDEED IT IS POSSIBLE TO CONSULT THE SIGNIFICANT CULTURAL HERITAGE OF THE LIBRARY ON INTERNET AND GAIN ACCESS TO HUNDREDS OF HISTORICAL TEXTS THAT HAVE BEEN DIGITIZED AND CAN BE BROWSED ON THE NETWORK, IN ADDITION TO THE SCIENTIFIC INDEXING OF THE COLLECTION OF PRINTS AND MENUS.

THIS AVANT-GARDE APPROACH AND THE PRESENCE OF A TEAM OF WORLD FAMOUS LECTURERS, WHO ARE OFTEN ASSISTED BY MUCH APPRECIATED VISITING CHEFS, GUARANTEE A VAST RANGE OF COURSES AS WIDE AS THE SUBJECTS ADDRESSED AND AT COMPETENCE LEVELS TO CATER FOR THE REQUIREMENTS OF PROFESSIONAL RESTAURANTEURS AS WELL AS ORDINARY COOKING ENTHUSIASTS. THE EXPERIENCE THAT IS SHOW-CASED IN THE CONTEXT OF THIS ARTICULATED TRAINING PORTFOLIO PROVIDES A UNIQUE LEARNING OPPORTUNITY: FROM PERSONALIZED TEACHING TO RAPID COURSES AND FROM THEME BASED MEETINGS TO STRAIGHTFORWARD CLASSROOM TEACHING. THERE ARE CELEBRITIES LIKE ETTORE BOCCHIA, MORENO CEDRONI, SCOTT CONANT, CARLO CRACCO, ALFONSO IACCARINO, GIADA DE LAURENTIIS, VALENTINO MARCATTILII, IGINIO MASSARI, GIANCARLO PERBELLINI, ANDREA ZANINI AND MANY OTHERS WHO ENDOW ALL ACTIVITIES WITH THE KNOWLEDGE THEY HAVE GAINED IN THE FIELD.

ACADEMIA BARILLA ALSO ORGANIZES CULTURAL MEETINGS AND OTHER INITIATIVES, AIMED AT APPRAISING THE SCIENCE OF COOKING, THAT ARE OPEN TO THE GENERAL PUBLIC WHERE EXPERTS, CHEFS AND FOOD CRITICS TAKE PART. MOREOVER, IT PROMOTES *PREMIO CINEMA* (CINEMA AWARD), AN AWARD FOR FILMS DEDICATED TO THE ITALIAN TRADITION IN FOOD AND COOKING.

The flavors of tradition in your own kitchen

FROM THE PEAKS OF THE ALPS AND THE COLD FOGGY PLAINS OF THE NORTH, ITALY EXTENDS AS FAR AS THE WARM DRY MEDITERRANEAN REGIONS OF THE SOUTH. THIS ENORMOUS VARIETY OF CLIMATIC AND ENVIRONMENTAL CHARACTERISTICS HAS CONTRIBUTED TO DEVELOPING A CUISINE THAT IS VERY MUCH ATTACHED TO THE TRADITIONS AND THE TYPICAL PRODUCTS OF THE VARIOUS REGIONS IN THE COUNTRY.

IN ADDITION, THE DIFFERENT HISTORICAL AND CULTURAL CONNOTATIONS OF EACH REGION – FOR EXAMPLE, THE AUSTRIAN INFLUENCE IN THE NORTH AND THE ARAB INFLUENCE IN SICILY – HAVE CAUSED ITS GASTRONOMIC CUSTOMS TO HAVE EVEN DEEPER ROOTS IN ITS HISTORY. THIS IS HOW THE FAMOUS DELICIOUS DISHES OF ITALIAN CUISINE CAME ABOUT; THROUGH THE SLOW PROCESS OF ADAPTING ANCIENT RECIPES THAT HAVE BEEN HANDED DOWN FROM GENERATION TO GENERATION.

FOR THIS REASON, DISCOVERING THE WEALTH OF ITALIAN CUISINE ENTAILS EMBARK-

INTRODUCTION

ING ON A JOURNEY THROUGH ITS REGIONS, IN ORDER TO UNCOVER THE INFINITE VA-
RIETY OF FLAVORS AND AROMAS THAT HAVE BEEN HANDED DOWN TO US, AS FRESH
AND AS GENUINE AS THE PRODUCTS OF A TRULY GENEROUS LAND.

IT IS THANKS TO THIS VARIETY AND THE RICHNESS OF THIS VAST CULINARY HERITAGE
THAT WE CAN EVEN SELECT QUICK AND EASY RECIPES THAT ARE WELL SUITED TO
TODAY'S FAST PACE OF LIFE WITHOUT SACRIFICING ANY OF THE FLAVORS. INDEED,
GASTRONOMIC TRADITION IS NOT ALWAYS CHARACTERIZED BY LONG COOKING
TIMES AND COMPLEX PREPARATION: SIMPLE AND FLAVORFUL RECIPES ARE TO BE
FOUND IN ALL REGIONS. AND THIS IS HOW *ACADEMIA BARILLA* CAME TO SELECT TWO
HUNDRED RECIPES OUT OF THE THOUSANDS AVAILABLE, IN ITS RICH GASTRONOMIC
LIBRARY, TO HAVE THEM TRIED OUT ONE BY ONE BY ITS *CHEFS*, IN ORDER TO OFFER
THE BEST OF QUICK AND EASY ITALIAN CUISINE, TO REVIVE THE FLAVORS AND ARO-
MAS OF TRADITION AND TO APPRAISE THE EXTRAORDINARY PRODUCTS OF VARIOUS

REGIONS, MAKING A CULINARY JOURNEY THE LENGTH OF THE PENINSULA, FROM THE ALPS TO THE MEDITERRANEAN.

THE CUISINE OF THE NORTHERN REGIONS IS VARIED AND HISTORICALLY IT WAS CHARACTERIZED BY THE INFLUENCE OF NUMEROUS MEDIEVAL COURTS. DISTINCTIVE TRAITS ARE THE WIDESPREAD USE OF BUTTER AND BACON FAT, THE WIDE VARIETY OF STUFFED PASTA AND EGG PASTA, WHICH BOAST ANCIENT NOBLE ORIGINS AND WHICH ARE ALSO DUE TO THE EXCELLENT PRODUCTION METHODS OF PORK AND SALAMI. THERE ARE ALSO MANY DELICACIES THAT MAKE THEIR WAY INTO THE RECIPES; FROM TRUFFLES TO MUSHROOMS, TO THE MANY TYPES OF CHEESE, TO CULATELLO AND HAM, ALL TO BE SAVORED WITH FULL BODIED WINES OR EVEN LIGHT SPARKLING WINES. THE TRADITIONAL SWEETS AND THE REGIONAL PRODUCTION OF CHOCOLATE AND *TORRONE* (NOUGAT) ARE OF PARTICULAR INTEREST.

THE CENTRAL, HILLY AND MOUNTAINOUS REGIONS FURROWED BY LONG VALLEYS ARE THE REALM OF MEAT. THIS IS WHERE THE GASTRONOMIC TRADITION BOASTS A WEALTH OF GAME, EXCELLENT BEEF AND A VERY OLD TRADITION IN THE PRODUC-

TION OF PORK, ALONGSIDE FIRST CLASS FAMOUS WINES. OLIVE OIL UNITES THE

RECIPES WITH SOFT FRUITY OVERTONES. THERE IS FISH TOO, WITH FAMOUS RECIPES

FROM THE COASTS.

THE SOUTHERN REGIONS BOAST A SUN-KISSED CUISINE, WITH MARKED MEDITER-

RANEAN CHARACTERISTICS, THE PREDOMINANCE OF INTENSELY FLAVORED OLIVE

OIL, FISH AND WINES THAT ARE FULL OF CHARACTER, WITH A HIGH ALCOHOL CON-

TENT. THIS IS THE LAND THAT SMELLS OF CITRUS FRUIT AND PRECIOUS FRAGRANT

ALMONDS. DURUM WHEAT SEMOLINA PASTA IS AT ITS BEST HERE, IN TERMS OF PRO-

DUCTION, CUISINE, THE DIVERSITY OF SHAPES AND TRULY UNIQUE DISHES. THIS IS

WHERE PIZZA ORIGINATED AND WHERE IT IS NOW MADE IN A VAST VARIETY OF FLA-

VORS. THE VARIETY OF CHEESE IS TRULY AMAZING.

DRAWING FROM THIS EXTRAORDINARY UNIQUE HERITAGE, ACADEMIA BARILLA HAS

COMPILED A SELECTION OF EASY DISHES THAT CAN BE PREPARED BY EVERYBODY.

THESE ARE RECIPES THAT CAN RECREATE, EVEN IN AN INSTANT, THE FLAVORS OF AN

OLD TRADITION.

APPETIZERS

Appetizers, in all their many colorful and delicious forms, made from the most varied and imaginative ingredients, in a lunch or dinner, have the fundamental role of introducing the style and the flavors of what will follow in the main courses of the meal.

The appetizer sets the tone of the meal, but it also serves the purpose of preparing the taste buds of the diner by stimulating the senses of sight, smell and taste with dishes that, more than any other, can tantalize the diner with an imaginative choice of ingredients and the alchemy of the preparation techniques.

Indeed, there are always appetizers at important banquets, but also for family celebration meals; nowadays appetizers are also used for various occasions at different times of the day to substitute a proper lunch with a brunch or a buffet or what in Italy is termed as a "happy hour" which is when savories are offered with drinks in a bar. Such simplified meals can go as far as to include a first course or indeed a whole meal, only a bit lighter and merrier.

THE INGREDIENTS USED TO PREPARE APPETIZERS ARE TYPICALLY THE MOST DISPARATE AND CAN VARY FROM COLD CUTS (INCLUDING ALL THE REGIONAL VARIATIONS), MEAT (INCLUDING GAME), FISH, EGGS, VEGETABLES AND EVEN FRUIT. THERE ARE RECIPES FOR HOT AND COOKED APPETIZERS, FOR COLD AND RAW ONES, AND RECIPES USING FRESH AS WELL AS PRESERVED INGREDIENTS. THE ITALIAN APPETIZER IS TYPICALLY A PLATE OF COLD CUTS (USUALLY TYPICAL OF THE REGION WHERE IT IS SERVED), OFTEN TOGETHER WITH VEGETABLES PRESERVED IN OIL OR VINEGAR, OR EVEN WITH FRESH FRUIT (A GOOD EXAMPLE BEING PARMA HAM WITH MELON, FIGS OR GRAPES). ALONGSIDE THESE TYPICAL ITALIAN APPETIZERS, THERE ARE THE MORE ELABORATE PREPARATIONS REPRESENTED BY A TERRINE OR PATÉ, OFTEN MADE OUT OF GAME AS A MAIN INGREDIENT, BUT SOMETIMES ALSO USING COLD CUTS, MEAT OR FISH, ACCOMPANIED WITH CRACKERS, VOL-AU-VENT OR SMALL PASTRY BOATS.

PIZZAS, STUFFED FOCACCIA AND PIES ALL FULFILL PERFECTLY WELL THE ROLE OF AN INTRODUCTION TO A MEAL AS EFFECTIVELY AS STUFFED PANZEROTTI, FRIED OR BAKED PASTA OR PASTIES MADE WITH PUFF PASTRY. FISH IS VERY WELL SUITED TO

BE PREPARED RAW, OR "IN CARPACCIO," ON CANAPÉS LIKE CAVIAR OR SLICES OF SMOKED FISH WITH FRESH BUTTER.

VARIOUS "COCKTAILS" ARE PREPARED WITH SHELL FISH BY PUTTING TOGETHER THE FLESH OF SHELL FISH WITH COLD SAUCES AND PRESENTING IT IN ELEGANT GOBLETS; OF COURSE, FISH IS THE MAIN INGREDIENT FOR SAVORY SEAFOOD SALADS, AND WE MUST NOT FORGET REFINED OYSTERS AND MORE HUMBLE MUSSELS AND THE INFINITE NUMBER OF RECIPES TO PREPARE THEM RAW OR COOKED. AMONG THE MORE ARTISTIC ENTRÉES THERE ARE THE GELATINE BASED ASPIC PREPARATIONS, ANOTHER INGREDIENT THAT IS OFTEN USED IN APPETIZERS, THAT PROVIDE FOR A PRETTY PRESENTATION OF VEGETABLES, FISH, WHITE CHICKEN OR TURKEY MEAT, MUSHROOMS AND EGGS. MUSHROOMS ARE ADDED RAW TO SALADS OR COOKED IN BÉCHAMEL SAUCE OR SOME OTHER WARM SAUCE AS A FILLING FOR VOL-AU-VENTS OR TO GO ON TOP OF CROSTINI. VEGETABLES ARE THE BASIS OF TASTY AND COLORFUL SALADS TOGETHER WITH FRESH OR DRIED FRUIT, COOKED MEAT OR HAM; OFTEN, VEGETABLES ARE PREPARED STUFFED AU GRATIN IN THE OVEN OR COLD AND UNCOOKED IN SUMMER.

APPETIZERS

Meat

Arancini di riso - *Rice balls*   22

Calcioni molisani   24
Molise Calcioni (savory stuffed fritters)

Frittata rognosa del Garda   26
Meat omelet Garda-style

La pastuccia   28
Pastuccia (Polenta with sausage and raisins)

Rosa carpaccio *Rose carpaccio*   30

Torta dolce salata *Sweet and savory pie*   32

Tortino di patate e formaggio   34
Potato and cheese pie

Vitello tonnato *Veal with tuna sauce*   36

Fish

Acciughe marinate al finocchio selvatico   38
Marinated anchovies with wild fennel

Capesante alla veneziana   40
Venetian-style scallops

Caponata con sgombri *Caponata with mackerel*   42

Carpaccio di tonno *Sicilian tuna carpaccio*   44

Frittelle di bianchetti *Whitebait fritters*   46

Granseola alla triestina   48
Trieste style spider crab

Insalata calda di polpo e patate   50
Warm salad with octopus and potato

Insalata di mare *Seafood salad*   52

Mozzarella in carrozza *Mozzarella in batter*   54

Polipetti affogati alla scarola riccia   56
Stewed baby octopus with escarole

Salsa verde *Salsa verde*   58

Sarde alla beccafico con tartare
di verdure e salsa alla menta   60
Sardines beccafico with vegetable tartar and mint sauce

Scapece de licette   62
Anchovies in a vinegar marinade

Zuppetta di cozze *Mussel soup*   64

Vegetable

Caprese con verdure saltate al timo   66
Caprese with sauteed vegetables with thyme

Carciofi alla Giudia *Artichokes Roman Jewish-style*   68

Ciambelle con formaggio *Cheese doughnuts*   70

Crema di zucca con mousse di caprino
e aceto balsamico di Modena   72
*Pumpkin puree with goat cheese mousse
and traditional balsamic vinegar of Modena*

Crocchette di Fontina *Fontina cheese rissoles*   74

Farinata *Chickpea-flatbread*   76

Fiori di zucca fritti *Fried zucchini flowers*   78

Gnocco fritto *Deep-fried pizza*   80

Insalata con pane carasau   82
Sardinian summer nuraghe

Panelle di fave *Broad bean fritters*   84

Panzanella *Panzanella (bread salad)*   86

Polpette con formaggio e uova *Cheese balls*   88

Polpette di melanzane *Eggplant "meatballs"*   90

Torta di patate *Potato cake*   92

Tramezzino Ticino   94
Ticino Style "tramezzino" (sandwich)

Vol-au-vent con radicchio e fonduta   96
Vol au vent with radicchio and fondue

Arancini di riso
Rice balls

Servings 10
Difficulty Medium
Region Sicily

Meat

For the Arancini: 2 lb (380 g) rice – ⅜ lb (200 g) breadcrumbs – 4 eggs – 3½ oz (50 g) butter – 4½ oz (80 g) grated Parmigiano Reggiano (Parmesan) cheese – salt – pepper – 1 pinch saffron.
For the filling: 7oz minced pork – 1 small onion – ½ cup (1 dl) white wine – 1oz (3 cl) extra virgin olive oil – 1oz (30 g) tomato concentrate – 3½ oz (50 g) peas – 4½ oz (60 g) Pecorino primo sale (sweet and soft sheep's milk cheese), chopped – 4 oz (60 g) caciocavallo cheese, grated – peanut oil for frying – pinch of saffron.

30 minutes preparation time + 5 minutes cooking time

Boil the rice in a quart of boiling salted water with a pinch of saffron. Cook over medium heat for about 15 minutes, stirring continuously until all of the water has been absorbed.

Remove from the heat and, in a large bowl, mix in with the beaten eggs, the butter and the Parmigiano Reggiano cheese.

Chop the onion, cook over a medium heat until soft. Add meat and fry lightly. Then add tomato concentrate and wine and cook until the wine evaporates. Add a drop of water, salt, pepper and cook for 20-30 minutes and then leave to cool. Add the boiled peas, the diced Pecorino and a little of the grated Caciocavallo.

In a saucepan over medium heat, add oil and meat sauce: mix it with the peas, salt and pepper and cook until sauce has reduced down by over half and is fairly dry.

Mix together the meat mixture, Pecorino primo sale (or Pecorino dolce cheese) and grated Caciocavallo cheese (or Parmesan cheese).

With moist, but not wet hands, form a 1 to 1½-inch ball of the rice mixture in the palm of one hand. Place some of the meat mixture in the hole and cover with rice, to make a ball the size of an orange. When all the balls are formed roll them in flour, then dip them in the beaten egg, followed by the breadcrumbs. Then fry the rice balls in very hot oil.

Calcioni molisani
Molise Calcioni (savory stuffed fritters)

Servings 6
Difficulty Medium
Region Molise

Meat

For the filling: 1 lb (400 g) ricotta cheese – 2 egg yolks – 3½ oz (100 g) ham – 3½ oz (100 g) spicy Provolone cheese – parsley – extra virgin olive oil – white pepper – salt.
For the pasta: 1 lb (400 g) all-purpose flour – 3½ oz (100 g) lard – 2 eggs – lemon juice – salt.

30 minutes preparation time + 5 minutes cooking time

In a bowl mix the ricotta with the yolks, add the ham and the roughly diced Provolone, put in the chopped parsley, add salt and season with freshly ground pepper. Mix well and form into a smooth ball, solid to the touch. Leave to rest in the bowl and meanwhile prepare the pastry, making a well in the flour on a cutting board and putting in the egg and a pinch of salt. Mix well (if it is too tough, add a little warm water). Using a rolling-pin, roll out a fairly thin sheet. On the sheet laid on the cutting board, arrange several little mounds of filling, the size of a large walnut, about 2 inches from one another.

Fill one sheet in this way, and then cover with the other one. Using a pastry-cutting wheel, cut out the "calcioni," pressing the edges lightly with the fingers, to fill the empty spaces. Pour the oil into a cast-iron frying-pan and, when it reaches boiling, fry the "calcioni" in batches, until they are golden. Remove with a skimmer, drain on absorbent kitchen paper and serve piping hot.

Local name: Caggiuni

Frittata rognosa del Garda
Meat omelet Garda-style

Servings 4
Difficulty Low
Region Veneto

Meat

5 eggs, fresh – 1 onion – 5 oz (150 g) minced meat – 1 stalk celery – 3½ oz (100 g) bacon – 2 tablespoons (3 cl) oil – 1 oz (20 g) butter – 2½ oz (70 g) Parmesan cheese, grated – salt and pepper to taste.

30 minutes preparation time + 10 minutes cooking time.

Add a drop of oil and the butter to a pan and place it over medium heat. Add finely chopped onion and celery. The celery should be boiled (whole) for about 15 minutes beforehand.

Then add the smoked pancetta cut into small pieces and add salt and pepper to taste.

Add the minced meat (this can be pork, mixed or a mixture of beef, veal and salame). Cook everything for at least 20 minutes.

Beat the eggs with the grated cheese until well mixed. Then stir eggs into the previously cooked meat.

Poor the mixture into a very hot, well greased frying pan. Once the bottom part of the frittata is cooked, flip and cook the other side. Serve on hot plates.

La pastuccia
Pastuccia (Polenta with sausage and raisins)

Servings 4
Difficulty Medium
Region Abruzzo

Meat

1 lb (500 g) cornmeal – salt to taste – ⅔ pint (300 g) water – 2 oz (60 g) raisins – 1⅓ lb (600 g) pork sausages, cut into small chunks – 3 egg yolks – 7 oz (200 g) pancetta (Italian bacon) – 2½ tablespoons (4 cl) extra virgin olive oil.

30 minutes preparation time + 40 minutes cooking time

Put the flour in a bowl with salt and mix in the warm water.
When everything is mixed well, so that no dry flour remains in the bottom of the bowl, add the raisins and sausage cut into pieces, mixing together with some egg yolks.
Then put a copper oven dish (or a non-stick pan) onto the heat with most of the diced pancetta and when it begins to brown, pour in the mixture, spreading it out and leveling it off with a wooden spoon, then spread a little clarified pork fat over the surface and sprinkle with pieces of pancetta.
Brown well top and bottom and serve piping hot.

Rosa carpaccio
Rose carpaccio

Servings 4
Difficulty Low
Region Veneto

Meat

14 oz (400 g) beef fillet – 4 oz (120 g) Parmigiano Reggiano cheese – 4 oz (120 g) artichokes – 3½ oz (100 g) champignon mushrooms – 2 lemons – 3½ oz (100 g) extra virgin olive oil – 4 oz (120 g) arugula (rocket salad) – salt and pepper to taste.

25 minutes preparation time

Clean the mushrooms and cut into regular slices. Clean the artichokes, removing hard outer leaves. Cut in half, remove the hairy choke and cut into thin slices and then season with 1oz (2.5 cl) oil, salt, pepper and lemon to prevent them turning black.

Arrange on a plate a layer of arugula which has already been washed and dried and season with a drizzle of oil. Place the artichokes wedges on it.

Arrange the finely sliced meat in a regular pattern on the plate.

Season the sliced mushrooms with ¾ oz (2 cl) oil, salt and freshly ground black pepper. Arrange on top of meat.

Garnish with flakes of Parmesan cheese.

Squeeze a lemon over the Rose Carpaccio and season with 1½ oz (50 g) oil, a little salt.

Chef's tips
Since mushrooms and artichokes tend to darken, we suggest seasoning them immediately after cutting with oil and lemon.

Torta dolce salata
Sweet and savory pie

Servings 4
Difficulty Low
Region Basilicata

Meat

For the pastry: 7 oz (200 g) all-purpose flour – 3½ oz (100 g) sugar – 3½ oz (100 g) butter – 1 egg yolk.
For the filling: 3 eggs – ¾ oz (20g) sugar – 4¼ oz (120 g) ricotta cheese – 2½ oz (70 g) Caciotta cheese, fresh – 2½ oz (70 g) Parma ham (in one slice) – 1 small mozzarella cheese – ½ oz grated Pecorino cheese – extra virgin olive oil – salt.

40 minutes preparation time + 1 hour cooking time

Mix 3½ oz (100 g) of sugar with the flour, put the mixture on a pastry board and make a well in it. Put the egg yolks into the well with a pinch of salt and the butter in pieces. Mix to obtain a soft and well amalgamated dough. Shape into a ball, cover and leave to rest, in a cool place, for an hour. Put the sieved Ricotta into a bowl, and blend in the diced Caciotta, Mozzarella and ham.
Mix well, then blend in the remaining ¾ oz (20 g) of sugar, a whole egg and a yolk and the Pecorino, and mix thoroughly.
Divide the dough into two parts, one large and one small.
Make two thin disks, and use the larger one to line a mold, greased with oil, going overlapping the edges. Fill with the stuffing, leveling off. Cover with the other disk, folding the edges of the lower one around it. Brush with some beaten egg and bake in a moderate oven at 350°F (180°C) for one hour.

Tortino di patate e formaggio
Potato and cheese pie

Servings 4
Difficulty Medium

Meat

1 ³/₄ lb (800 g) potatoes – 6 ⅓ oz (180 g) Parma ham – 6 ⅓ oz (180 g) grated Parmigiano Reggiano cheese – 6 ⅓ oz (180 g) Emmental cheese – salt – 1 ³/₄ oz (50 g) butter.

15 minutes preparation time + 1 hour cooking time

Boil the potatoes in salted water, then peel them and cut them in rather thin slices. Grease an oven dish, arrange a layer of potatoes in it, on top of the potatoes put the ham cut into slices, Emmental and Parmesan cheese.
Continue to make layers of potatoes, ham, Emmental and Parmesan until all the ingredients are used up. Finally, put a few small touches of butter on the top and bake in the oven at 350°F (180°C) for about 30 minutes.

Did you know that...
There is a wide variety of types of potato, but they can generally be classified in two categories: white and yellow fleshed potatoes. The white ones are fairly floury and are used to make puddings, mashed potatoes and gnocchi, while the yellow potatoes, rich in vitamin A, are best boiled, fried or roasted.

Chef's tips
The potatoes should be immersed in cold, salted water and should not be peeled before cooking so that they do not lose the majority of the nutrients.

Vitello tonnato
Veal with tuna sauce

Servings 4
*Difficulty **Medium***
*Region **Piemonte***

Meat – Fish

1⅓ lb (600 g) veal round – 1 oz (30 g) stale bread – 1¾ oz (50 g) vinegar – ½ lb (250 g) drained tuna – ⅛ oz (5 g) capers – ½ cup (1 dl) extra virgin olive oil – 1 clove of garlic – ½ cup (1 dl) white wine – 2 anchovies – 3 hard-boiled eggs – rosemary – sage – meat broth.

20 minutes preparation time + 25 minutes cooking time

Salt the veal round and brown in a frying pan, in the oil, over a high heat. Remove from the heat and place the veal in an oven dish, add the garlic and herbs and cook in the oven at 180-200°C (350-390°F) for about 15 minutes so that the veal is still slightly pink inside. When the veal is cooked, remove from the oven-dish and deglaze the cooking juices with the white wine.

Reduce the liquid and then add the capers and the desalted anchovies, the tuna and the stale bread which has been soaked in wine vinegar and squeezed dry. Cook for a few minutes then liquidize with the yolks of the hard boiled eggs and the broth necessary to make the desired consistency of the sauce.

Slice the veal roast and serve with the tuna sauce.

Did you know that...
Capers can be found in most Mediterranean countries. They were known and sought after even in Ancient times and were even mentioned in the Bible as an aphrodisiac.

Chef's tips
One of the most famous caper varieties is that of Salina, a small volcanic island located off the coast of Sicily in the Aeolian archipelago.

Acciughe marinate al finocchio selvatico
Marinated anchovies with wild fennel

Servings 4
Difficulty Low
Region Latium

Fish

1 lb 5oz (600 g) fresh anchovies – 3oz (90 g) yellow onion – 1 clove of garlic – rind of ½ a lemon – 2½ oz (8 cl) extra virgin olive oil – 1 glass of dry white wine – wild fennel – thyme – bay leaf – parsley – coriander – salt – pepper.

40 minutes preparation time + 24 hours to marinate

Carefully clean the anchovies, remove the entrails, the head and the fish bones. Place in a lightly oiled dish, season the anchovy fillets with salt and pepper. Cook in the oven for 5 min at 400°F (200°C). Remove the anchovies from the oven.

In a pan, soften the thinly sliced onion in a little oil. Pour a little white wine in the pan, add lemon juice, garlic, wild fennel, thyme, a little coriander and the bay leaf. Cook over low heat, stirring occasionally.

Sprinkle the finely chopped parsley, orange and lemon rind into the pan and cook for a further 5 minutes. Arrange anchovies on a plate, pour the marinade over them and leave in refrigerator for 24 hours.

Leave at room temperature for 15 minutes before serving.

Chef's tips
Fresh anchovies can also not be cooked at all and left to marinate uncooked. Clearly, uncooked anchovies will need to be left to marinate for longer.

Capesante alla veneziana
Venetian-style scallops

Servings 4
Difficulty Low
Region Veneto

Fish

8 scallops – ⅛ oz (5 g) garlic – ½ oz (15 g) parsley – 1oz (30 g) extra virgin olive oil – 1 sprig dill – ⅛ oz (5 g) lemon juice – salt and pepper to taste.
20 minutes preparation time + 5 minutes cooking time

Carefully brush the shells when still shut. Wash repeatedly, the open to prepare for the cooking, remove the yellow part and keep the white part clean.
Heat the oil in a pan, add finely chopped garlic and the mussels.
Over a high flame, add parsley and dill. Season with salt and pepper and cook for 5 minutes.
Re-arrange each shell by placing two mussels inside and pouring a little of the cooking liquid over each one.

Did you know that...
Capesanta (scallop) is Italian for Coquille Saint-Jacques, the symbol of pilgrims on their way to Santiago de Compostela in Spain. It is also one of the symbols in Pope Benedict XVI's coat of arms It is often linked to the image of Venus, for instance in the famous Botticelli's painting "The birth of Venus."

Chef's tips
The secret of this dish lies in the freshness of the scallops. It can be served hot or cold and can be accompanied by hot croutons brushed with garlic.

Caponata con sgombri
Caponata with mackerel

Servings 4
Difficulty Low
Region Campania

Fish

4 crisp round bread croutons – 14oz (400 g) cauliflowers, cleaned – 5oz (150 g) pickled mixed vegetables (Giardiniera or Jardinière) – 2 pickled Neapolitan peppers – 1 head escarole – 1 head lettuce – 3½ oz (100 g) capers – 3½ oz (100 g) black olives – 4 salted anchovies – 7oz (200 g) mackerel – 3½ oz (100 g) extra virgin olive oil – 3½ oz (100 g) vinegar, white – 3½ oz (100 g) white wine – lemon juice – ground pepper -salt.
20 minutes preparation time

In a large salad bowl put the anchovies, boiled cauliflower (in boiling water with salt and the lemon juice), jardinière, pickled Neapolitan peppers, escarole and lettuce, all chopped, and the capers and olives. Season with a pinch of salt, pepper, oil and vinegar, and mix well.
In a container soak the "freselle" (crisp round bread croutons) in the vinegar and wine; once softened, crumble rather roughly into the salad bowl and mix well, leveling off the top.
On the top arrange the boiled mackerel dressed with oil and lemon juice.

Carpaccio di tonno
Sicilian tuna carpaccio

Servings 4
Difficulty Low

Fish

½ lb (250 g) fresh tuna, thinly sliced – 4 tablespoons lemon juice – 4 tablespoons extra virgin olive oil – 1 celery heart, cut à la julienne, – 3 ½ oz (100 g) olives, sliced – salt and pepper to taste – 4 basil leaves – 2 slices bread.

15 minutes preparation time

Arrange the tuna slices on a platter.

Season with lemon, salt and pepper; marinate for five minutes.

Combine the drained olives with celery, basil. Top the Carpaccio and serve with warm bread croutons.

To make croutons: rub bread with extra virgin olive oil, salt and pepper.

Grill or toast in the oven until slightly brown.

Frittelle di bianchetti
Whitebait fritters

Servings 4
Difficulty *Low*
Region **Calabria**

Fish

1 lb (500 g) whitebait – 10½ oz (300 g) flour – ⅔ cup (1.5 dl) water – 1 small bunch of parsley – ½ oz (40 g) extra virgin olive oil for frying – salt – black pepper.

10 minutes preparation time + 10 minutes cooking time

Wash the whitebait thoroughly but gently and put in a bowl with batter prepared beforehand by mixing the flour, water, salt, chopped parsley and ground black pepper.
Put the olive oil in a frying pan on a medium to high flame. When the oil is hot, put spoonfuls of the whitebait into the boiling oil. When the fritters are cooked, drain on kitchen roll.
Sprinkle salt to taste and serve hot.

Did you know that...
This dish is traditionally called "Crispeddi'i'nunnata."
"Nunnata" is made up of tiny fish that are almost still at the larval stage of development (sounding like neonata (newborn), it means just born and hence "nunnata" in the dialect of Reggio and "rosamarina" in the dialect of Cosenza).

Granseola alla triestina
Trieste style spider crab

Servings 4
Difficulty Low
Region Friuli
Venezia Giulia

Fish

½ onion – juice and grated zest of 1 lemon – 3½ oz (100 g) breadcrumbs – 1 oz (30 g) butter – 1⅓ tablespoons (2 cl) olive oil - parsley – 1 spider crab, or 1 lb 1⅝ oz (500 g) crab-meat.

15 minutes preparation time + 10 minutes cooking time

Cook the spider crab in a large pot of boiling water for 10 minutes. Drain and leave to cool.
Remove the claws and open them with a nutcracker, removing the meat and placing it in a bowl.
Using a knife and a pair of scissors, open the shell of the crab, starting with the underside.
Remove all of the meat, and mix it in the bowl with the claw meat. Then, tear it all into smaller pieces.
Alternatively, you can use canned crab-meat. In this case, drain and break into pieces.
Finely chop the onion and sauté in the butter with the breadcrumbs, parsley, and if you have it, the roe. Remove from the heat and add the juice and the grated lemon zest. Then add the oil and the crab-meat. Stir together and then use as a spread on toasted bread or crostini.

Did you know that...
Although crabs can be found almost everywhere, that they are originally from China.

48

Insalata calda di polpo e patate
Warm salad with octopus and potato

Servings 4
Difficulty **Medium**

Fish

1 ½ lb (I kg) octopus – ½ lb (250 g) potatoes, boiled – 1 ½ oz (4 cl) extra virgin olive oil – ½ lemon – parsley – salt and pepper.

10 minutes preparation time + 40 minutes cooking time

Clean the octopus removing internal organs, eyes and beak. Wash the octopus thoroughly under cold running water. Put the octopus in a large pan full of water, add salt and bring to the boil.
Cook the octopus for at least half an hour, until, pricking it with a fork, it is tender but does not break.
Drain, and if you prefer, remove skin while still hot; otherwise leave to cool and cut into pieces.
Peel and dice the potatoes and boil in salted water with a little white vinegar
When the potatoes are cooked, mix with the octopus and season with salt, lemon juice, oil, chopped parsley and pepper. Serve.

Did you know that...
The potato plant originated in South America, especially in Chile and Peru where it has been cultivated for at least 4 thousand years. It was imported to Europe in the 16th century by the Spaniard Pizzarro but the tasty tuber met with great diffidence, to the extent that for several centuries it was considered to be the carrier of illness.

Insalata di mare
Seafood salad

Servings 4
Difficulty **Medium**
Region **Campania**

Fish

2½ lb (1 kg) mussels – 1⅓ lb (600 g) clams – ⅔ lb (300 g) cocktail shrimps – ⅔ lb (300 g) baby octopus – ⅔ lb (300 g) baby squid – 1 carrot – 1 celery stalk – 1 small onion – rosemary – marjoram – thyme – 1 lemon – 1 teaspoon strong French mustard – 1 cup extra virgin olive oil – 2 cloves of garlic – plenty of parsley.

35 minutes preparation time

Brush and wash the mussels thoroughly. Rinse the clams under running water several times. Open the mussels and the clams separately over high heat without seasoning, in a covered pot. Save the cooking liquid and strain. Shell the mussels and the clams.

Put them into a pot with 4.2 cups (1 liter) of water, with the chopped herbs and the vegetables (onion, celery, carrot, rosemary, marjoram, thyme). Boil for 20 minutes and strain.

Add the shrimps to the stock. Boil for 3 minutes and peel them. Filter the stock through a very fine sieve.

In the seafood stock, boil the baby octopuses (previously cleaned and washed) and the baby squid (previously cleaned and cut into rings). Drain them. Cut the baby octopuses into small pieces.

Arrange the mussels, clams, shrimp, baby squid and baby octopuses on a large serving dish.

Make a sauce with 3½ oz (100 g) oil, a teaspoon of mustard, the juice of one lemon (or more if necessary), the whole or chopped cloves of garlic, a generous amount of chopped parsley, salt and pepper.

Beat with a fork and pour over the fish. Mix, cover and keep in a cool place for at least 30 minutes.

Mozzarella in carrozza
Mozzarella in batter

Servings 4
Difficulty Low
Region Latium

Fish

8 slices of bread- 8 slices mozzarella cheese – 8 anchovies, in oil – 1 egg – all-purpose flour – extra virgin olive oil – milk.

30 minutes preparation time + 5 minutes cooking time

Remove the crust from the slices of bread and soak them lightly in the milk.

Between two slices of bread put two slices of Mozzarella and two anchovy fillets.

Press together so that the sandwich sticks well.

Dip the edges in beaten egg with a little milk and then fry in abundant oil, turning them so that they are golden all over.

Serve hot.

Did you know that...
This is a traditional recipe for appreciating in a very simple way the goodness of mozzarella that is rendered particularly tasty by adding anchovies.

Polipetti affogati alla scarola riccia
Stewed baby octopus with escarole

Servings 4
Difficulty **Medium**
Region **Campania**

Fish

For the stewed baby octopuses: 12 baby octopuses each weighing approximately 3 oz (80 g) – ½ cup (1 dl) extra virgin olive oil – ½ cup (1 dl) dry white wine – 1 oz (30 g) garlic – 7 oz (200 g) cherry tomatoes – 1¾ oz (50 g) parsley – salt and pepper to taste.
For the escarole: 1¼ lb (600 g) escarole – 3½ oz (100 g) black olives – 1 oz (30 g) capers – ¼ cup (6 cl) extra virgin olive oil – salt and pepper to taste.

25 minutes preparation time + 1 hour cooking time

Wash and clean the baby octopuses and cut the tentacles in pairs. Heat the oil in a saucepan over a medium heat, when it is hot add the octopuses and cook them for about 5 minutes. Add the diced tomatoes, garlic, chopped parsley, cook for a further 10 minutes and season with salt and pepper.

Sauté, stirring occasionally and add white wine little by little. Cook over a low heat (around 30 minutes).

Clean and wash the escarole, chop up into large pieces. Heat oil in a frying pan over a medium heat, when the oil is hot, add the escarole and fry gently for a few minutes. Then add some black pitted olives and the capers.

Season with salt and pepper. Cover and cook on low heat. Serve the escarole with the octopus.

Chef's tips
Wash the baby octopus in salty water so that they do not produce foam while cooking.

Salsa verde
Salsa verde

Servings 4
Difficulty **Low**
Region **Emilia Romagna**

Fish

2 tablespoons (150 g) parsley, finely chopped – 2 tablespoons white bread crumbs soaked in vinegar – 1 clove of garlic – 1 teaspoon capers – 1 anchovy – 1 boiled egg – vinegar – extra virgin olive oil – salt.

10 minutes preparation time

Pass the soft part of a bread loaf through a sieve, chop the capers and anchovy and mix with parsley and garlic, adding oil and vinegar to taste. Use freshly-chopped parsley and do not leave too long before using it: if you leave it too long it will ferment and acquire a strong flavor.
Serve with boiled meat.

Sarde alla beccafico con tartare di verdure e salsa alla menta
Sardines beccafico with vegetable tartar and mint sauce

Servings 4
Difficulty Medium
Region Sicily

Fish

2¼ lb (1 kg) sardines – 3½ oz (100 g) breadcrumbs – 1½ oz (40 g) desalted anchovies – 1½ (40 g) oz raisins – 1 oz (30 g) pine nuts – 1¾ oz (50 g) parsley – 3 oz (80 g) extra virgin olive oil – ⅓ oz (10 g) sugar – bay leaves to taste.
For the tartar: 1¾ oz (50 g) carrots – 1¾ oz (50 g) zucchini – 1¾ oz (50 g) sweet peppers – 3½ oz (100 g) extra virgin olive oil.
For the sauce: ¾ oz (20 g) mint – 1½ oz (40 g) extra virgin olive oil.

25 minutes preparation time + 15 minutes cooking time

Remove scales, and clean the sardines. Wash taking care to leave the fillets attached. Sauté the breadcrumbs in a little oil in a saucepan. Once brown, add chopped anchovies, pine kernels, and raisins which have been soaked in water. Add chopped parsley to the mixture, crushed bay leaf, and season with salt and pepper. The mixture should be well blended but not too liquid.

On the oven tray place a tin mold lined with grease proof paper. Place sardine fillets inside the tin mold pressing them evenly to the sides. Pour the mixture into the mold. Press the mixture lightly down and cover it by joining the sardines. Put the mold in oven at 350°F (180°C) for 10 minutes.

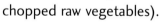

Serve the dish after seasoning with oil and parsley, accompanied with the mint sauce and the vegetable tartar (with the finely chopped raw vegetables).

Scapece de licette
Anchovies in a vinegar marinade

Servings 4
Difficulty Medium
Region Molise

Fish

1 lb (500 g) anchovies – 3½ oz (100 g) durum wheat flour – frying oil.
For the Marinade: 1 clove of garlic – 2 cups white wine vinegar – 1 cup water – 5 sage leaves – salt.

45 minutes preparation time + 15 minutes cooking time

Wash the baby anchovies gently in a colander, drain them and coat in flour. Heat abundant oil in a pan and, as soon as it is very hot, fry the anchovies. When they are golden, remove with a slotted spoon, salt, and arrange them in a glass or earthenware salad bowl, sprinkling each layer with sage leaves and chopped garlic.

In a pan boil the vinegar with the water and a pinch of salt and pour the liquid while still hot, but not boiling, onto the anchovies. They are excellent after a few days. Young anchovies – to be eaten whole – are only available in the spring. They can be substituted by baby sardines and therefore "scapece" can be prepared all year round.

Did you know that...
Scapece (from the Arabic "iskebegh") is a way to prepare, and even preserve, fried foods. This style of preparation of Arab origin generally consists in soaking the fried ingredient in vinegar, garlic and herbs. During the Middle Ages, it was a technique used throughout a large part of southern Italy and even became a favorite dish of Holy Roman Emperor Frederick II.

Zuppetta di cozze
Mussel soup

Servings 4
Difficulty *Low*

Fish

4½ lb (2 kg) mussels – ⅔ cup (1.5 dl) extra virgin olive oil – 2 cloves of garlic – 2 tablespoons parsley chopped- ⅔ cup (1.5 dl) white wine – chili (optional) – salt and pepper – 12 slices of bread, toasted.

15 minutes preparation time + 10 minutes cooking time

Put a large pot, with the oil, on a medium heat. Add 1 garlic clove, finely chopped and some parsley. Allow flavors to blend for a few minutes, then add the wine, salt and pepper.
After 5 minutes, add the mussels, previously washed. Cover the pot and cook until all have opened.
Rub the remaining garlic on the toasted bread. Arrange the bread slices in the bowls and pour over the mussels with their sauce.
If so desired, some hot chili pepper can be added to the sauce and the parsley can be sprinkled over the mussels just before removing them from the heat.

Caprese con verdure saltate al timo
Caprese with sauteed vegetables with thyme

Servings 4
Difficulty Low
Region Campania

Vegetable

¾ lb (320 g) buffalo-mozzarella cheese – ½ lb (250 g) tomatoes, red ripened – ⅜ oz (10 g) basil, fresh – 3½ (5 cl) tablespoons extra virgin olive oil – ⅛ oz (5 g) oregano – ⅛ oz (5 g) salt – ⅛ oz (2 g) pepper – 4oz (120 g) zucchini – 3oz (80 g) celery – 3oz (80 g) peppers – ⅛ oz (5 g) thyme.

25 minutes preparation time + 15 minutes cooking time

Dice the vegetables. Heat oil in a pan, quickly sauté the celery, add the peppers then the zucchini. Season with salt and pepper and thyme. Cook for a few minutes, stirring regularly. In the meantime, thinly slice the tomatoes and the mozzarella.

Place slices of tomato and of mozzarella alternately on a plate, and arrange the sautéed vegetables with thyme in the middle.

Finally, decorate with fresh basil leaves and oregano.

Add salt to the vegetables once cooked, so that they do not release their liquid during cooking.

Chef's tips
This dish is easy to serve in summer thanks to the seasonal ingredients used: vegetables.

Carciofi alla Giudia
Artichokes Roman Jewish-style

Servings 4
Difficulty Medium
Region Latium

Vegetable

4 artichokes – 3½ cups (8dl) extra virgin olive oil – salt and pepper – lemon juice.
20 minutes preparation time + 20 minutes cooking time

Remove the hard leaves from the artichokes, cut stalk leaving about 1.2 inches of it.
With a very sharp small knife, shape the artichoke from top to bottom turning it, so as to remove only the hard part of the leaves. Soak the artichoke in water with the juice of one lemon and repeat the operation for each single artichoke. Meanwhile, in a pan heat up plenty of oil.
Drain the artichokes, dry them and press them lengthwise on the table to open the leaves. Each operation must be repeated for each single artichoke.
Season the inside of the artichokes with salt and pepper. Then dip the artichokes into the boiling oil with the stalk up, cook per about 10 minutes, then turn them upside down and cook on the other side, for the same time.
Drain them on straw or absorbent paper and serve hot.

Did you know that...
The artichoke is a plant which originates in the countries of the Mediterranean. Botanists believe that it derives from a wild thistle and was first cultivated by the Etruscans.

Ciambelle con formaggio
Cheese doughnuts

Servings 4
Difficulty **Medium**
Region **Umbria**

Vegetable

1 ¾ lb (800 g) bread dough – 4oz (120 g) Pecorino cheese, sweet – 3 tablespoons extra virgin olive oil – oil for greasing the oven tin.

20 minutes preparation time + 20 minutes cooking time

Grate half the Pecorino and break the other half into pieces. Work the *bread dough* with the cheese and the oil, form into a loaf and let it rise.

Make several doughnuts from the dough (roll dough into a sausage shape first then join the ends), arrange them on a greased baking sheet not too close to one another and allow to rise once more for a further 30 minutes. bake in a hot oven at 400°F (200°C) for about twenty minutes.

Allow to cool before serving.

Did you know that...
Usually ciambelle are made with dough made from flour and yeast to which either savory or sweet ingredients may be added to give it the desired flavor. Precisely for this reason, ciambelle are probably one of the Italian recipes with the most variations to the extent that they are prepared in a different way in every city.

Crema di zucca con mousse di caprino e aceto balsamico di Modena
Pumpkin puree with goat cheese mousse and traditional balsamic vinegar of Modena

Servings 4
Difficulty Low
Region Emilia Romagna

Vegetable

2½ lb (1 kg) pumpkins – 1 lb (350 g) goat cheese, fresh – ½ cup fresh cream – 2 sprigs rosemary – nutmeg to taste – 4 sprigs chives – Academia Barilla Monti Iblei DOP Extra Virgin Olive Oil to taste – salt and pepper to taste – few drops of Academia Barilla Traditional Balsamic Vinegar of Modena, aged 12 years.

20 minutes preparation time + 60 minutes cooking time

Cut the pumpkin into eight sections and place on a baking sheet. Add rosemary, drizzle with a little olive oil and a little salt. Bake at 320°F (160°C) for about 1 hour. If you like, you can cut one of the sections into very thin slices to fry and turn into chips for the garnish.

While the pumpkin is baking, prepare the goat cheese mousse: in a bowl, mix together the goat cheese with the cream, a little olive oil, salt and freshly ground black pepper.

Mix well using an immersion blender. Then, place in the refrigerator.

Chop the chives and put to one side.

Once the pumpkin is cooked, remove from the oven and leave to cool. Using a large kitchen spoon, scrape out the flesh. Add nutmeg, a little extra virgin olive oil and salt and pepper to taste. Mix well with a fork or pass through a sieve until smooth.

With the help of a round pasta mold, spoon the pumpkin purée onto the center of the plate. On top of the pumpkin, place two scoops of goat cheese mousse using two spoons.

Garnish with the pumpkin chips, chives, a couple drops of aged Traditional Balsamic Vinegar of Modena and freshly ground black pepper, to taste.

Crocchette di Fontina
Fontina cheese rissoles

Servings 4
Difficulty Medium

Vegetable

2 oz (20 g) all-purpose flour – 2 oz (20 g) rice flour – 1 lb (500 g) Fontina cheese – 5 oz (150 g) butter – 1 cup milk – 4 egg yolks – 2 eggs – salt and pepper to taste – nutmeg to taste – frying oil.

20 minutes preparation time + 15 minutes cooking time

Melt the butter in a small pan. Add the two types of four and the milk. Bring to the boil to make a bechamel mixture. Remove from the heat and add the diced Fontina and then heat until it melts. Once the Fontina has melted, add the two eggs and the yolks and mix rapidly. Add salt, pepper and nutmeg.
Then remove from the heat and transfer the mixture to a dish to cool.
Once cold, prepare small round croquettes and dip them, one by one, in the beaten egg and then bread crumbs.
Fry in abundant oil.

Farinata
Chickpea-flatbread

Servings 4
Difficulty Low
Region Liguria

Vegetable

1 lb (400 g) chickpea flour – 4 cups water – ½ cup extra virgin olive oil – salt to taste – pepper to tastez.

10 minutes preparation time + 20 minutes cooling time + 12h dough resting time

Put water and chickpea flour in a bowl and whisk to blend, season with salt to taste and leave to rise for twelve hours. Then remove any foam with a spoon and stir the mixture.

Pour a little oil into a large shallow tin, covering the bottom completely, then pour in the mixture through a sieve, and stir with a wooden spatula so that the mixture absorbs the oil. Sprinkle the very finely chopped onion and freshly-ground black pepper on top.

Bake in a hot oven at 425°F (220°C), for about twenty minutes, until golden brown. Serve warm.

Did you know that...
"Farinata" is a chickpea based "focaccia" that is typical of the city of Genoa.
In 1284, a Genoese ship was returning from the victorious battle of Meloria against the fleet of Pisa when it got caught in a storm. The storage room of the ship had been filled with chickpeas and other provisions and after the storm passed, the sailors checked to see what was left of their supplies. Apparently, saltwater had entered the storage room creating a sort of chickpea puree. Having nothing else to eat, the sailors fed themselves the mush, which in the meantime had turned into a sort of bread, extremely tasty, due to the heat of the sun and once they reached land, they decided to replicate the dish, calling it "farinata."

Fiori di zucca fritti
Fried zucchini flowers

Servings 4
*Difficulty **Low***

Vegetable

15 zucchini flowers – 7oz (200 g) all-purpose flour – 1 egg – ½ cup (1dl) water – frying oil – salt and pepper.

5 minutes preparation time + 5 minutes cooling time

In a bowl mix the flour with the egg and the water, stirring until the batter reaches the right texture (when dipped in it, the flower should be covered in a thin coating).
Wash the flowers, removing the pistil, drain and dry them gently. Heat abundant oil in a pan over a medium/high flame. Dip the flowers in the batter, turn them gently and, when the oil is very hot, fry them, a few at a time, then, once nicely golden, drain them on a sheet of kitchen paper.
Sprinkle over some salt, arrange them on a plate and serve immediately.

Did you know that...
Zucchini flowers are also excellent with a sprinkling of sugar.

Gnocco fritto
Deep-fried pizza

Servings 4
Difficulty Low
Region Emilia Romagna

Vegetable

1 lb (500 g) all-purpose flour – 1½ oz (40 g) lard – ⅔ oz (20 g) fresh yeast – pinch baking soda – 1 cup (2.5 dl) milk – ⅓ oz (10 g) salt.

10 minutes preparation time + 3 minutes cooking time

Mix everything with the warm milk, cover with a cloth and leave to rise for about 1 hour, at room temperature.

Roll out to a thickness of about 0.4 inch, cut dough into diamond shapes and fry in the lard.

Serve hot to accompany or stuffed with cold meats and cheese.

Did you know that...
This dish is traditionally also called "Crescentina" or "Torta fritta" (Fried cake).

Insalata con pane carasau
Sardinian summer nuraghe

Servings 4
Difficulty Medium
Region Sardegna

Vegetable

6 slices carasau bread – 5 oz (150 g) cherry tomatoes, thinly sliced – 5 oz (150 g) spring onions – 5 oz (150 g) radishes – (150 g) 5 oz cucumbers – 1 oz (30 g) extra virgin olive oil – 3 oz (90 g) Pecorino cheese, in slivers – fresh chives, to garnish.

30 minutes preparation time

Dip the bread into a bowl of water and leave until it starts to soften.

When the bread has softened, cut it into 16 squares or circles with a diameter of 2 to 3 inches.

Season all the vegetables with salt and pepper to taste and drizzle with a little of the oil.

Place 1 Carasau round in the center of a plate.

Arrange tomato slices on top of the round of Carasau in one layer, overlapping them slightly.

Top with another cracker (Carasau) and arrange radish slices on top in the same manner.

Top with another round and a layer of cucumber slices and shallots, followed by another cracker.

Arrange the Pecorino on top and around the stack.

Drizzle remaining olive oil over the stack and on the plate and sprinkle the plate with the chopped chives.

Did you know that...
Pane carasau is also known as "carta musica" (music sheet) due to its resemblance to the parchment paper that sacred music was written on.

Panelle di fave
Broad bean fritters

Servings 4
*Difficulty **Medium***
Region Sicily

Vegetable

2¼ lbs (1 kg) broad beans, soaked in water overnight and boiled – water – salt – 1 onion, cut into thick slices – wild fennel – olive oil – frying oil – chili peppers (optional).

2 hours and 30 minutes preparation time + 5 minutes cooking time

Soak the dried broad beans overnight. The morning after, boil in salted water, along with an onion cut into thick slices and a few wild fennel tops. Cook for a long time, at least 2 – 3 hours, so that the broad beans become a puree.

Sieve and place the thick mixture on a marble board or a flat, well-greased cooking surface. Roll the mixture out into an even sheet about 0.8 inch (2 cm) thick using a rolling-pin. Allow to cool and cut into strips: the so called "panelle" must be deep-fried in hot oil.

Serve hot. If desired sprinkle with crushed chili to taste.

Panzanella
Panzanella (bread salad)

Servings 4
Difficulty Low
Region Toscana

Vegetable

1 lb (400 g) home-made bread – 2 tomatoes, ripened – 2 red onions – 1 cucumber (optional) – 1 sprig basil – extra virgin olive oil – vinegar – salt and pepper.

30 minutes preparation time

Cut the bread into slices and soak in cold water for a few minutes. Once they are well soaked, remove a little bread at a time and squeeze out excess water using your hands. Then break apart into small, dry crumbs.

Place in a salad bowl and add tomatoes, cucumbers and sliced onion and basil leaves. Dress with oil, salt and pepper and move to a cool place. When it is time to serve, add a splash of wine vinegar.

Did you know that...
A "noble" version of panzanella seems to have been served to Vittorio Emanuele, the King of Italy, by statesman Bettino Ricasoli, in 1865. At the time, the King was a guest in Ricasoli's castle in Chianti for a hunting trip. The green of the basil, the white of the bread and the red of the tomato, recalled the colors of the newborn Italian Kingdom.

Polpette con formaggio e uova
Cheese balls

Servings 4
Difficulty *Low*
Region *Abruzzo*

Vegetable

⅔ lb (300 g) white bread crumbs – 1 tablespoon parsley, chopped – 1 clove of garlic, chopped – 5 eggs – ½ cup (1 dl) extra virgin olive oil – 7 oz (200 g) grated Pecorino semifresco cheese (slightly aged cheese).

20 minutes preparation time + 5 minutes cooking time

In a bowl, mix the breadcrumbs, the Pecorino cheese and the eggs.
Complete the mixture by adding the garlic and parsley and form the cheese balls to be fried in hot olive oil.
The "polpettine" (cheese balls) can be served like this, or with a tomato sauce, in which case they should be cooked for a further fifteen minutes in the sauce.

Did you know that...
According to legend, polpette (cheese balls or meat balls for that matter) were invented in the court of Genghis Khan by an Italian doctor who had fled from Italy where he was persecuted because he had married a Jewish lady.

Polpette di melanzane
Eggplant "meatballs"

Servings 4
Difficulty Low
Region Calabria

Vegetable

1 lb (450 g) eggplant – 1 egg – 3½ oz (100 g) breadcrumbs – 1 teaspoon of parsley, chopped – 1 clove – 1 clove of garlic – 4 basil leaves – 1¾ oz (50 g) Pecorino cheese – frying oil – salt and pepper.

1 hour preparation time+ 5 minutes cooking time

Wash the eggplants, cut them in half, put into a pot and cover with water. Bring to the boil and leave to cook for about 45 minutes, drain, and leave to cool.

Prepare separately the bread crumbs with chopped garlic, parsley and basil, the grated cheese and the salt.

Squeeze out the excess liquid from the eggplants and mash them with the bread crumbs and the whole egg, amalgamating everything well so as to obtain a uniform mixture.

With this mixture, prepare some elongated, fairly flat "meatballs," and fry them in the oil.

These may be served hot or cold.

Did you know that...
This version of traditional meatballs, made with eggplant rather than meat, is a typical Italian appetizer and is quite easy to prepare.

Chef's tips
These may be served with a spicy tomato sauce as a side dish.

Torta di patate
Potato cake

Servings 4
Difficulty Low
Region Trentino
Alto Adige

Vegetable

8 medium sized potatoes – 3 tablespoons (40 g) all-purpose flour – lard or oil –
salt.

20 minutes preparation time + 30 minutes cooking time

Choose some mature potatoes, peel them and grate into a large bowl with a cheese grater. Add the
flour and a pinch of salt and mix well.
Transfer this mixture to an oven-dish greased with lard or abundant oil, and bake in a preheated hot
oven about 400°F (200°C). Bake for about 30 minutes until the surface is nicely golden and crisp.

Chef's tips
Instead of a potato cake, you can also
prepare some excellent "tortelli," by
using the same same mixture to make
flat rounds to fry in plenty of oil.

Tramezzino Ticino
Ticino Style "tramezzino" (sandwich)

Servings 4
Difficulty Low

Vegetable

8 slices bread – 3 oz (80 g) mayonnaise – 4 oz spicy Gorgonzola cheese – 8 walnut kernels – 1 pear.

15 minutes preparation time

Stack the slices of bread one on top of the other and use a knife to cut off the crust from the four edges. Grind the walnuts, slice the gorgonzola into thin slices, and lastly slice the pear.
Spread mayonnaise on all the slices of bread, and on four of them place the Gorgonzola slices, then the pear slices, the ground walnuts and then cover with the remaining slices of bread.
Cut in half diagonally and place the sandwiches on a moist tea towel, then cover with another damp tea towel to avoid the sandwiches drying up.
Keep them covered until serving.

Did you know that...
A tramezzino is the Italian version of the British sandwich. The sandwich spread from England to Italy at the beginning of the 20th century, reinterpreted by the Futurists and by D'Annunzio as "traidue" ("between the two") and later became the tramezzino.

Vol-au-vent con radicchio e fonduta
Vol au vent with radicchio and fondue

Servings 4
Difficulty Low
Region Veneto

Vegetable

12 vol au vents – 6 oz (170 g) Fontina cheese – 1 ¼ cups (3 dl) milk – 2 egg yolks – 2 teaspoons all-purpose flour – black truffle (optional) – 10½ oz (300 g) red radicchio – salt to taste.

10 minutes preparation time + 15 minutes cooking time

Beat the egg yolks with 2 tablespoons of milk. Chop up the Fontina into chunks. Blend the flour into the remaining milk and add the Fontina to the mixture. Transfer the mixture to a pan and cook over a medium heat, whisking vigorously with a metal whisk so that the mixture thickens.
Add the egg yolks and continue to cook for about 10 minutes. Season with salt and keep the mixture warm. Wash the radicchio and chop it finely and then add it to the cheese mixture.
Fill the vol au vents with the mixture and serve. They can be garnished with some freshly-grated black truffle on top.

Did you know that...
Radicchio can be found throughout Italy. There are many types of this bitter, leafy vegetable, but the most famous is probably the late-season radicchio Tardivo di Treviso.
Italians began cultivating this variety, a rather labor-intensive process, in the middle of the 16th century.

FIRST COURSES

SINCE REMOTE TIMES, FIRST COURSES HAVE BEEN THE MAIN, IF NOT THE ONLY DISH SERVED IN A MEAL; THE TRADITION OF WHAT IN ITALY IS CALLED A "MINESTRA" (A SOUP) WITH VEGETABLES AND PULSES DATES BACK CENTURIES AND HAS OFTEN DEFINED WITH ITS NAME, THE CUSTOMS OF THE POPULATION OF A SPECIFIC REGION (THE NEAPOLITAN "MANGIA FOGLIE" OR LEAF EATERS OR THE FLORENTINE "MANGIA FAGIOLI," OR BEAN EATERS, ...). MINESTRE, ARE USUALLY CLASSIFIED AS "DRY" OR "IN BROTH" AND ARE DISTINGUISHED, LIKE ALL OTHER DISHES IN ITALY, BY REGIONAL OR LOCAL TRADITIONS IN THE PREPARATION OF THE MOST DISPARATE INGREDIENTS. OFTEN THESE RECIPES START OFF WITH CEREALS THAT ARE EITHER COOKED IN THEIR ORIGINAL "WHOLE GRAIN" FORM (THERE ARE MANY RECIPES FOR RISOTTO, TYPICAL OF NORTHERN ITALY; FARRO SOUPS; BARLEY SOUP OR "ORZOTTI" FROM THE ITALIAN WORD FOR BARLEY WHICH IS "ORZO"), OR ALTERNATIVELY THEY ARE GROUND AND USED AS SEMOLINA OR FLOUR COOKED IN WATER ("POLENTA," MADE WITH DIFFERENT TYPES OF CORNMEAL AND ALSO WITH FLOUR MADE FROM OTHER CEREALS, IS THE BEST EXAMPLE). IT IS ALSO CEREALS THAT ARE USED TO MAKE THE BLEND OF FLOUR AND WATER TO CREATE DRY PASTA (THE PASTA THAT

TODAY IS PRODUCED MAINLY ON AN INDUSTRIAL SCALE). THERE IS A GALAXY OF "MACCHERONI" – THIS IS THE "HISTORICAL" TERM GENERALLY USED TO INDICATE ALL THE TYPES OF SHAPED PASTA – WITH MORE THAN ONE HUNDRED DIFFERENT SHAPES AND JUST AS MANY RECIPES: PASTA WITH TOMATO SAUCE, PESTO, BOLOGNESE SAUCE, VEGETABLES, MEAT, GAME, FISH AND CHEESE; DRESSED WITH SAUCE, "PASTICCIATA" (ALL MIXED UP ROUGHLY WITH OTHER INGREDIENTS), AU GRATIN OR COOKED IN THE OVEN. THERE IS NO OTHER INGREDIENT IN THE WORLD WHICH LENDS ITSELF TO SO MANY DIFFERENT METHODS OF COOKING AND SO MANY EVER NEW VARIATIONS AND CULINARY INVENTIONS. FRESH PASTA IS MADE WITH A MIXTURE OF SOFT WHEAT FLOUR AND EGGS. IT ALSO HAS INNUMERABLE TRADITIONAL FORMS: LASAGNE, TAGLIATELLE, TAGLIERINI, MALTAGLIATI, PAPPARDELLE... BUT FRESH PASTA IS ALSO THE BASIS OF ALL STUFFED PASTA (TYPICAL OF FESTIVE MEALS): TORTELLINI, AGNOLOTTI, ANOLINI, CAPPELLETTI, PANSOTTI, RAVIOLI... ADDING BOILED POTATOES, PUMPKIN COOKED IN THE OVEN, FINELY CHOPPED BOILED SPINACH, CHEESES LIKE RICOTTA, STALE BREAD SOAKED IN MILK, VARIOUS OTHER VEGETABLES AND EGGS, TO FLOUR, IS WHAT GIVES RISE TO VARIOUS

TYPES OF SO CALLED "GNOCCHI," ONE OF THE ORIGINAL SHAPES OF PASTA, AND PROBABLY FOR THIS REASON, TO BE FOUND ALL OVER ITALY. WHEN CEREALS ARE NOT THE MAINSTAY OF THE DISH, THE INGREDIENTS MOST OFTEN USED ARE UNDOUBTEDLY VEGETABLES: INDEED THERE ARE THOUSANDS OF WAYS OF PREPARING MINESTRONE AND SOUPS WITH THE PRODUCE OF THE VEGETABLE GARDEN: RANGING FROM THE SO CALLED "PAPPA COL POMODORO" TOMATO SOUP (OF LITERARY AND POPULAR MUSIC FAME), TO PASTA WITH BEANS, GENOESE AND MILANESE MINESTRONE, TUSCAN SOUP AND THAT OF NAPLES AND ROME... ALL OF THEM ORIGINALLY HUMBLE DISHES AND, PRECISELY FOR THAT REASON, OFTEN ENRICHED WITH FRUGAL ADDITIONS OF LARDO, BACON OR PIG'S CHEEK, MUSHROOMS OR CHICKEN LIVERS AND GIBLETS, GARLIC AND ONION, HERBS AND VARIOUS FLAVORINGS. OFTEN, SIMPLE AND EASILY DIGESTIBLE INGREDIENTS GO A LONG WAY TO ENRICH A GOOD MEAT BROTH: PASSATELLI, STRACCIATELLA, VARIOUS TYPES OF PASTINA (SMALL PASTA), ALL MADE WITH EGGS AND CHEESE AND RENDERED TASTIER AND MORE SUBSTANTIAL, FROM TIME TO TIME, WITH THE ADDITION OF SOME BREADCRUMBS, PARSLEY OR OTHER TIDBITS.

FIRST COURSES

Bucatini all'amatriciana
Bucatini with amatriciana sauce

Servings 4
Difficulty Low
Region Latium

Meat

1 lb (400 g) bucatini – 7 oz (200 g) bacon – 4 tomatoes, ripe – 3 leaves of basil –
2 cloves of garlic – 1 chilli pepper, red (or 2 dried ones) – 3 tablespoons (4 cl) extra
virgin olive oil – 1½ oz (40 g) Pecorino Romano cheese, grated – salt and pepper.

15 minutes preparation time + 12 minutes cooking time

Slice the bacon and dice finely. Heat a pan over a medium heat, add the oil and the bacon and fry gently.

Blanch the tomatoes for 20 seconds, peel them, remove the seeds and dice. Add the chopped garlic to the bacon and fry gently for a few seconds. Then add the tomato, the chilli, the chopped basil, salt and pepper. Cook for ten minutes.

Cook the pasta in boiling salted water until it is cooked "al dente," drain and dress with the sauce and the Pecorino Romano cheese.

Did you know that...
Amatriciana sauce takes its name from Amatrice, a small town in the
Latium region in the Province of Rieti.

Fettuccine con salsiccia e porri
Fettuccine with Italian sausage and leeks

Servings 4
Difficulty Medium

Meat

8 teaspoons (4 cl) extra virgin olive oil – 10½ oz (300 g) pork sausages – 2 leeks, thinly sliced – ½ cup (1 dl) white wine – ¾ oz (20 g) butter – salt to taste – black pepper to taste – 13 oz (360 g) fettuccine – 1¾ oz (50 g) grated Parmigiano Reggiano cheese – 2 tablespoons parsley, chopped.

15 minutes preparation time + 15 minutes cooking time

Bring a large pot of water to boil.

Remove casing from sausage and fry gently in the oil. Wash leeks, chop finely and add to sausage. Cook for a few minutes and then add the white wine. Cook until the liquid reduces. Season with salt and black pepper; simmer and add a drop of water.

Cook the pasta in a large pan of salted water. Drain the pasta when it is cooked "al dente" and sauté it in the sauce with a little of the cooking water from the pasta. Add a little butter.

Sprinkle with grated Parmigiano Reggiano cheese and garnish with parsley before serving.

Did you know that…

Leeks are one of the few ingredients that were considered a fundamental source of nutrition during periods of famine in the Middle Ages. Leeks have been consumed since ancient times: even if we do not have the exact date of when they were discovered, there is no doubt that they were cultivated 4,000 years ago along the banks of the Nile.

From the Nile Valley, leeks spread to the Mediterranean coasts, becoming extremely popular in ancient Rome, where the Roman Emperor Nero was given the nickname "il porrofago" (or leek eater) due to his habit of eating a lot of leeks to clear his voice.

Linguine con frutti di mare
Linguine with sea food sauce

Servings 4
Difficulty Medium
Region Abruzzo

Fish

14 oz (400 g) linguine – 1 lb 1½ oz (500 g) mussels – 3½ oz (100 g) baby squids – 1 lb 1½ oz (500 g) clams – 3½ oz (100 g) baby cuttlefish – 3½ oz (100 g) prawn tails – 1 oz (30 g) tomato paste – 3⅜ tablespoons (5 cl) extra virgin olive oil – 1 tablespoon parsley, chopped – 1 clove of garlic – chili pepper – salt to taste.

30 minutes preparation time + 20 minutes cooking time

Put the oil into a pan with the garlic, chili and chopped parsley, and the tomato paste, which has been diluted in a little warm water, over a medium heat. Fry gently and when it begins to color, add the baby calamari and cuttlefish.

Cook over medium heat for a few minutes and then add the peeled scampi, the mussels and the clams, and season with a pinch of salt. Cover and cook until the mussels and clams are open.

Cook the pasta in plenty of salted boiling water. Drain when the pasta is cooked "al dente." Toss the pasta in the sauce.

Maccheroni con le sarde alla siciliana
Macaroni with sardines

Servings 4
Difficulty *Low*
Region *Sicily*

Fish

14 oz (400 g) macaroni – 5⅓ oz (150 g) sardines – 3⅜ tablespoons (5 cl) extra virgin olive oil – 1 bunch wild fennel – 3 cloves of garlic – ⅓ oz (10 g) chopped onion – ⅔ oz (20 g) desalted anchovies – ⅓ oz (10 g) raisins – ⅓ oz (10 g) pine nuts – ½ tablespoon parsley – 1 pinch saffron – salt and pepper.

5 minutes preparation time + 30 minutes cooking time

In a pan, put 2 tablespoons of oil, 2 cloves of garlic and few tablespoons of cold water, a touch of saffron, diluted with a drop of water, and season with salt and pepper. Cook for about 4 minutes. Add the sardines that have been washed and filleted and continue to cook for a few minutes. Remove the garlic and put to one side.

For the sauce: sauté in a few tablespoons of oil, 1 clove of garlic and the chopped onion. Add the fennel which has been blanched and chopped, the raisins, pine nuts, the anchovies which have been crushed to a purée in the mortar with the parsley and diluted with a ladleful of cooking water from the fennel and cook over a medium heat for a few minutes.

Cook the pasta in the boiling salted cooking water of the fennel. Drain when the pasta is cooked "al dente" and arrange in an oven-dish alternating with layers of sauce and sardines, ending with a layer of sauce. Bake in a medium oven for about 20 minutes and serve.

Pappardelle al sugo di lepre
Pappardelle with hare sauce

Servings 4
Difficulty Medium
Region Tuscany

Meat

For the pasta: 14⅛ oz (400 g) flour – 4 eggs.
For the sauce: 14⅛ oz (400 g) hare, boned – 1½ oz (40 g) carrots – 1½ oz (40 g) onions – 1½ oz (40 g) celery – ½ cup (10 cl) red wine – ½ cup (10 cl) milk – 1¾ oz (50 g) tomato sauce – 2¾ teaspoons (40 g) extra virgin olive oil – 1¾ oz (50 g) grated Parmigiano Reggiano cheese – salt and pepper.

2 hours preparation time + 30 minutes cooking time

Make a well in the flour, add the eggs and mix until you obtain a uniform dough. Leave to rest for 20 minutes. Roll out the pasta into fairly thin sheets, flour them lightly and fold them over and over again and then cut the pappardelle with a knife so that they are about ¾ inch (2 cm) wide. Spread the pappardelle out on a lightly floured tray to dry. Chop the carrot, onion and celery finely.
Cut the hare into pieces. Heat a large pot, preferably an earthenware pot, add the oil and fry the vegetables gently. When they have softened, add the meat and fry thoroughly. Pour in the wine and simmer until the liquid reduces. Season with salt and pepper. Add the tomato sauce and the milk. Cook, adding a little warm water if necessary. Remove the pieces of hare from the pot, mince and put back over the heat and cook for 5 minutes.
Cook the pasta in boiling water, drain when it is cooked "al dente" and dress with the sauce. Sprinkle with grated Parmesan cheese and serve immediately.

Spaghetti aglio, olio e peperoncino
Spaghetti with garlic, oil and chili

Servings 4
Difficulty Low
Region Latium

Vegetable

14⅛ oz (400 g) spaghetti – 4 cloves of garlic – ½ cup (1 dl) extra virgin olive oil – chili pepper, seedless – parsley – salt.

5 minutes preparation time + 12 minutes cooking time

Cook the pasta in abundant salted water and drain when cooked. While it is cooking, sauté the garlic and the chili, without letting them burn, then pour over the cooked pasta, sprinkling some finely chopped parsley on top, if you like.

Spaghetti alla carbonara
Spaghetti with carbonara sauce

Servings 4
Difficulty *Low*
Region *Latium*

Meat

14⅛ oz (400 g) spaghetti – 5⅓ oz (150 g) pork cheek or bacon – 4 egg yolks – 3½ oz (100 g) Pecorino cheese – 1⅓ tablespoons (2 cl) extra virgin olive oil – salt and pepper to taste.

10 minutes preparation time + 5 minutes cooking time

Beat the egg yolks with a pinch of salt and a little Pecorino cheese in a bowl. Cut the bacon into strips, and sauté in a large pan. Cook the pasta in salted boiling water and drain when it is cooked "al dente." Put it into the pan and toss with the bacon. Remove from the heat and add the eggs, a little of the cooking water and mix for about 30 seconds. Mix in the remaining Pecorino cheese and serve immediately.

Did you know that…
According to the most widely accepted theories, the name "carbonara" is linked to the presence of ground black pepper. In the traditional recipe, it blackens the pasta so that it appears to be covered by coal (carbone) dust.

Spaghetti alla chitarra
Spaghetti alla chitarra

Servings 4
Difficulty Medium
Region Abruzzo

Meat

For the pasta: 14⅛ oz (400 g) durum wheat flour – 4 eggs.
For the sauce: 4 tablespoons (6 cl) extra virgin olive oil – 3½ oz (100 g) veal – 1¾ oz (50 g) pork – 1¾ oz (50 g) wether meat (mutton) – ¼ cup (5 cl) red wine – 14⅛ oz (400 g) tomato sauce – 2⅛ oz (60 g) Pecorino cheese, grated – 1 chili, dried – salt to taste.

40 minutes preparation time + 12 minutes cooking time

Roll out the pasta into sheets ⅛ inch (3mm) thick. Cut the pasta into sheets the same width as the chitarra (pasta guitar). Rest the floured sheets on the chitarra and roll the rolling pin over it pressing rather than spreading the pasta. This movement cuts the pasta into square cut spaghetti. Leave the spaghetti on a lightly floured tray to dry. Heat the oil in a large pan over a medium heat and when it is hot, add the chopped onion and sauté. Raise the heat and add the various types of minced meat and fry gently, add the wine and cook until it reduces completely. Add the tomato sauce and cook for about 15 minutes. Season with salt and add the flaked chilli. Cook the pasta in salted boiling water, drain when it is cooked "al dente." Add the sauce, the grated Pecorino cheese and serve.

Did you know that...
The instrument for cutting the pasta is called a "Chitarra abruzzese" (carrature in dialect). It has a rectangular wooden frame with steel strings placed very close together, with about 1mm between them, pegs to keep the strings taught and a surface where the pasta falls. This instrument in all its simplicity and perfection is what brings pasta alla chitarra or the typical square cut pasta to life.

Spaghetti alla Gennaro
Spaghetti Gennaro

Servings 4
Difficulty Low
Region Campania

Fish

14⅛ oz (400 g) spaghetti – 3½ tablespoons (5 cl) extra virgin olive oil – 3 slices stale bread – 4 desalted anchovies – 6 basil leaves – 3 cloves of garlic – 1 tablespoon oregano.

7 minutes preparation time + 8 minutes cooking time

Rub the bread slices with 1 clove of garlic, then crumble them onto a plate. Gently fry 2 whole cloves of garlic with the crumbled bread over a medium heat in half of the oil. Remove from the heat before the garlic becomes too brown. In another pan, put the rest of the oil, the chopped anchovies and the oregano. Gently fry for 2 minutes. Cook the spaghetti and drain when it is cooked "al dente." Quickly mix in the anchovy sauce, the crisp breadcrumbs and the roughly chopped basil. Serve immediately.

Did you know that…
It is a humble dish and it captures the Neapolitan spirit that Totò portrayed many times on the big screen and on the stage.

Spaghetti alla "gricia"
Spaghetti gricia (with bacon)

Servings 4
Difficulty *Low*
Region *Latium*

Meat

14⅛ oz (400 g) spaghetti – 3½ tablespoons (5 cl) olive oil – 10½ oz (300 g) pork cheek or bacon – fresh chilli pepper to taste – 5 oz (140 g) grated Pecorino cheese.

10 minutes preparation time + 10 minutes cooking time

Sauté the diced bacon and chilli in the oil in a large pan over a medium heat for 3 minutes. Cook the spaghetti in boiling salted water and drain when it is cooked "al dente." Mix in the sauce, sprinkle with Pecorino cheese and serve.

Spaghetti alla Norma
Spaghetti alla Norma

Servings 4
Difficulty Medium
Region Sicily

Vegetable

14⅛ oz (400 g) penne – 8¾ oz (250 g) eggplant – 2¾ oz (80 g) salted ricotta – 7 oz (200 g) tomato pulp/canned tomatoes – 1¾ oz (50 g) onion – 2 tablespoons (3 cl) extra virgin olive oil – 6 basil leaves – 1 clove of garlic – salt and pepper to taste.

30 minutes preparation time + 15 minutes cooking time

Cut the eggplant into cubes and lightly salt. Leave them for about 20 minutes so that all the water inside drains away. Flour and fry in plenty of olive oil. Chop the onion and garlic and put in a large frying pan over a medium heat. Add the oil and when it is hot, sauté the onion and garlic.
Add the eggplant, tomato pulp, salt and pepper and cook for about 15 minutes.
Meanwhile, cook the pasta in salted boiling water, drain when it is cooked "al dente" and mix in the sauce.
Add the basil and grated salted ricotta. Serve hot.

Did you know that...
Pasta all Norma is a recipe which originates in Catania and embodies typical Mediterranean flavors. The story goes that Nino Martoglio, a Sicilian writer and poet, was so impressed when he first tasted this dish that he compared it to "Norma" the famous opera by the composer, Bellini from Catania. And this tasty pasta dish has been known by the name of Pasta alla Norma ever since.

Chef's Tips
Before frying vegetables, it is best to slice them, place them in a colander and sprinkle with salt. In this way, the liquid contained in the vegetables is removed and the vegetables will be more crunchy and sweeter.

Spaghetti alla puttanesca
Spaghetti with puttanesca sauce

Servings 4
Difficulty Low
Region Latium

Fish

14⅛ oz (400 g) spaghetti – 4 desalted anchovies, pounded in a mortar with a pestle – 4 cloves of garlic, thinly sliced – 5⅓ oz (150 g) black olives – 1 tablespoon salted capers, rinsed and roughly chopped – 1 tomato – 1 tablespoon parsley, chopped – salt.

20 minutes preparation time + 10 minutes cooking time

Melt the butter and olive oil in a skillet over a medium heat. Then add the thinly sliced garlic and pounded anchovies. When the garlic begins to turn golden, add the olives, capers and the tomato which has already been peeled, the seeds removed and cut into thin slices.
Cook over high heat for 2 minutes. Season with salt. Cook the pasta in salted boiling water and drain when it is cooked "al dente." Toss the pasta in the sauce, sprinkle with parsley and serve.

Spaghetti al tonno fresco
Spaghetti with tuna

Servings 4
Difficulty *Low*
Region *Sicily*

Fish

14⅛ oz (400 g) tuna – salt – 2½ cups (6 dl) tomato sauce – 2 tablespoons parsley, chopped – 14⅛ oz (400 g) spaghetti – ⅞ cup (2 dl) extra virgin olive oil.
Variation: drained tuna – garlic.

Preparazione 15' – Cottura 15'

Cut the tuna into small chunks. Heat two thirds of the oil in a pan over a high flame and when it is hot, fry the tuna. Drain and keep warm.

Heat the rest of the oil over a medium heat, add the tomato sauce and cook for about 5 minutes. Add the fried tuna and season with salt. Cook for about another 5 minutes.

Meanwhile cook the pasta in plenty of salted boiling water and drain when it is cooked "al dente." Add the tuna sauce and sprinkle with parsley.

A variation of the recipe: 4 cups of tomato sauce, 10⅛ oz (300 g) canned tuna in oil, drained and chopped into small pieces.

Mix the ingredients, add some chopped parsley and a chopped garlic clove, and leave to cook over a low heat for 10 minutes, then use to dress the *spaghetti*.

Spaghetti cacio e pepe
Spaghetti with cheese and pepper

Servings 4
Difficulty Low
Region Latium

Vegetable

14⅛ oz (400 g) spaghetti – 2¾ tablespoons (4 cl) extra virgin olive oil – 3½ oz (100 g) grated Pecorino cheese – 1 heaped tablespoon pepper, ground in mortar – salt.

5 minutes preparation time + 10 minutes cooking time

Cook the pasta in salted boiling water. Drain when it is cooked "al dente." Add the extra virgin olive oil, the grated Pecorino cheese, the pepper and a ladle of cooking water from the pasta. Mix well and serve.

Tagliatelle al ragù
Tagliatelle with bolognese sauce

Servings 4
*Difficulty **Medium***
*Region **Emilia Romagna***

Meat

For pasta: 14⅛ oz (400 g) "00" flour – 4 eggs.
For the sauce: 14⅛ oz (400 g) Bolognese meat sauce – 2⅛ oz (60 g) grated Parmigiano Reggiano cheese.

30 minutes preparation time + 10 minutes cooking time

Place the flour on a flat work surface and form a well. Break the eggs into the center and begin to work the dough. Knead until smooth, and then let the dough rest for 20 minutes.
Roll out the dough into a thin sheet, flour lightly and fold it over onto itself a couple of times. Use a knife to cut ¼ in (5 mm) wide tagliatelle. Spread out the pasta on a lightly floured tray to dry.
Heat the ragù alla Bolognese in a large pan over low heat. Cook the tagliatelle in salted boiling water and drain when it is cooked "al dente." Toss with the ragù and sprinkle with grated Parmigiano Reggiano before serving.

Trenette al pesto
Trenette with pesto

Servings 4
Difficulty Low
Region Liguria

Vegetable

14⅛ oz (400 g) trenette – 1 oz (30 g) basil – ½ oz (15 g) pine nuts – 1 clove of garlic – ½ pint (2 dl) Ligurian extra virgin olive oil – 2⅛ oz (60 g) grated Parmigiano Reggiano cheese – 1½ oz (40 g) grated seasoned Pecorino cheese – salt and pepper to taste.

10 minutes preparation time + 10 minutes cooking time

For the "Pesto alla Genovese," chop the garlic and the basil and add a pinch of salt in order to preserve the green color of the basil leaves. Put the chopped basil and garlic in a mortar together with the pine nuts and crush with a pestle, adding a few drops of oil to obtain a so called "Pesto" or a paste. Transfer the paste into a bowl and mix in the rest of the ingredients (the cheese and the oil). Cook the "linguine" in abundant salted boiling water and strain when they are cooked "al dente." Dress with the "Pesto" sauce and, should it be too thick, dilute it slightly with a glass of pasta cooking water. Serve immediately.

Canederli di spinaci
Spinach canederli or spinach knodel (bread balls)

Servings 4
Difficulty **Medium**
Region **Trentino Alto Adige**

Vegetable

6 bread rolls – 3½ oz (100 g) spinach – 2 tablespoons Parmigiano Reggiano cheese – 3 eggs – 1 onion – 2⅔ oz (75 g) all-purpose flour – olive oil – salt and pepper.
For the dressing: 5⅓ oz (150 g) butter – 3½ oz (100 g) Parmesan cheese, grated.

25 minutes preparation time + 8 minutes cooking time

In a pan gently fry the finely chopped onion in the oil together with the diced bread. Meanwhile, in a bowl mix the boiled chopped spinach, eggs, flour and grated cheese, then season with pepper and salt. Add the sautéed onion and bread. Mix thoroughly and form some "canederli" (bread balls) to be cooked in boiling salted water for about 7-8 minutes.
Drain, pour on melted butter, sprinkle with Parmesan cheese and serve.

Did you know that...
Knodel are bread gnocchi (bread balls or dumplings) which are typical of Alto Adige. This is a typical first course which can be served either in broth or alone. It is considered a humble dish because traditionally it was made with stale bread.

Canederli tirolesi
Tirolese canederli
(traditional dumpling soup)

Servings 4
Difficulty **Medium**
Region Trentino
Alto Adige

Meat

7 oz (200 g) home-made bread – 7 oz (200 g) milk – 3½ oz (100 g) speck (smoked raw ham) – 3 oz (80 g) all-purpose flour – 2 eggs – ¾ oz (20 g) parsley – ⅛ oz chives – 4¼ cups (1 lt) broth – nutmeg to taste – salt to taste.

20 minutes preparation time + 15 minutes cooking time

Trim dry brown crusts from the bread. Cut the soft inner part into regular-sized cubes.
Put the cubes in a bowl, add the speck, chives, parsley, nutmeg and beaten eggs. Add the milk and allow to soften. Then blend to make a compact mixture. Add some flour to the mixture, to dry up any superfluous moisture. Season with salt and pepper. Knead the dough and, using two spoons, make some "quenelle," small balls the size of a walnut. Bring the meat stock to the boil, toss in the "canederli" and let them cook for 15 minutes, making sure that the stock boils gently so that the canederli do not break.

138

Cavatelli, rughetta e patate
Cavatelli with rocket and potatoes

Servings 4
Difficulty *Low*
Region *Apulia*

Vegetable

14 oz (400 g) cavatelli – 5⅓ oz (150 g) rocket – 5⅓ oz (150 g) canned tomatoes – 5⅓ oz (150 g) potatoes – 1 teaspoon extra virgin olive oil – 1 clove of garlic – 4 leaves of basil – salt and pepper.

20 minutes preparation time + 30 minutes cooking time

Sauté sliced garlic in a couple of tablespoons of oil, add basil and tinned tomatoes, a pinch of salt, then cook over a low heat.

Meanwhile, bring salted water to the boil in a large pot and boil the peeled and diced (about 1 in/3 cm cubes) potatoes. When almost done, add some rocket which has already been washed, and, once the water is boiling again, the cavatelli. Once cooked, drain, put everything back into the pot then add the tomato sauce. Serve hot.

Gnocchi di patate
Potato gnocchi

Servings 4
Difficulty Low
Region Emilia Romagna

Vegetable

14⅛ oz (400 g) flour – 2¼ lb (1 kg) potatoes – 2 eggs – 3½ oz (100 g) grated Parmesan cheese – salt to taste.

20 minutes preparation time + 30 minutes cooking time'

Boil the potatoes, peel and put them through a food mill.

Make a well in the flour and put in the potatoes and the eggs and mix together. With the dough make long rolls the width of a finger. Cut the rolls into lengths of 1 inch (2-3 cm).

In this way you will obtain small cylinders that you will then slide over the prongs of a fork, pressing slightly with your finger.

Cook the gnocchi in abundant salted water, drain and dress with a generous helping of butter and Parmesan cheese.

The gnocchi can also be served with tomato sauce or even better, with fresh cherry tomatoes which should be sautéed in butter first.

Gnudi profumati agli odori dell'orto
Vegetable dumplings

Servings 4
Difficulty *Medium*
Region *Latium*

Vegetable

For the gnudi: 14 oz (400 g) spinach, fresh – 7 oz (400 g) ricotta cheese, fresh – 1 oz (30 g) Parmigiano Reggiano cheese – 1 egg yolk – 5¼ oz (150 g) all-purpose flour – 1½ oz (40 g) potato starch – nutmeg to taste.
For the sauce: ½ cup (1 dl) tomato sauce – 2 oz (60 g) butter – ⅓ oz (10 g) sage.

30 minutes preparation time + 10 minutes cooking time

Cook the spinach in a small amount of boiling salted water, drain it and leave to cool completely. Drain and then chop finely.

On a work top, add all the other ingredients to the spinach purée, and mix everything together thoroughly and rapidly. The resulting mixture must be uniform and soft. Leave the mixture to rest for a short while on a well-floured board. With the aid of a pastry bag with a smooth ¾ inch (2 cm) nozzle, form some lengths of pasta and cut them into 1¼ inch (3 cm) long pieces.

Cook the "gnudi" in abundant salted water, and when they rise to the surface, strain them. In a large pan, melt the butter with the sage leaves. Lay the "gnudi" gently in the pan and toss them with the Parmesan cheese.

Arrange the "gnudi" on the serving dish, and decorate with fresh tomato sauce and some basil leaves.

Chef's Tips
The spinach must always be cooked in boiling salted water because in this way it maintains its green color.

Insalata di fusilli con verdure e calamari
Fusilli pasta salad with vegetables and squid

Servings 4
Difficulty **Low**

Fish

14 oz (400 g) fusilli – 2 carrots – 2 zucchini – 2 artichokes – 3 squids – bunch of aromatic herbs – ¼ cup (6 cl) extra virgin olive oil – juice of 1 lemon – salt – white pepper.

15 minutes preparation time + 10 minutes cooking time

Wash the carrots and peel them. Clean the zucchini and dry them.
Remove the tough outer leaves from the artichokes. Cut them in half lengthwise and eliminate the "choke" to be found in the center. Cut them into narrow strips and leave to soak in water with the lemon juice to avoid them turning black. Then cut the carrots and zucchini into narrow strips.
Clean the squid removing the skin from the sac and separating the tentacles from the body, and then eliminate the entrails and the transparent inner cartilage. Remove the beak located in the center of the tentacles and also the eyes. Then cut into very thin strips.
Cook the pasta in a pan of salted boiling water. Five minutes before it is cooked, add the vegetables to the water with the pasta. Stir and cook for 3 minutes, then add the squid for the last 2 minutes. When the pasta is cooked "al dente," drain, add a little oil, transfer everything to a tray and leave to cool. When it is cool, dress with the rest of the oil and lemon juice. Season with salt and white pepper. Serve on a bed of fresh Swiss chard.

Did you know that …
The first "artichoke queen," elected each year in Castroville, in California during the annual Artichoke Festival, was Marilyn Monroe in 1949.

Malloreddus
Malloreddus (Sardinian pasta)

Servings 4
Difficulty Medium
Region Sardinia

Meat

For the pasta: 14 oz (400 g) durum wheat flour – 1 cup (2.4 dl) – 1⅓ tablespoons (2 cl) extra virgin olive oil.
For the sauce: 3½ oz (100 g) lardo (bacon fat) – 3½ oz (100 g) minced lean veal – 3½ oz (100 g) minced lean pork – 14 oz (400 g) tomato sauce – 2⅔ oz (75 g) spicy Pecorino cheese, grated – 1 onion – 1 tablespoon parsley, chopped – 1 scant tablespoon rosemary, chopped – 2⅔ tablespoons (4 cl) extra virgin olive oil – salt and pepper.

40 minutes preparation time + 1 hour cooking time

Mix a generous tablespoon of oil into the semolina with a pinch of salt and a little water in order to obtain a soft but consistent mixture.

Divide into pieces, shape into 0.8 inch (2 cm) diameter sticks and cut these to a length of 1.2 inches (3 cm). Make a hollow with your thumb, and line them up, floured, on a pastry board.

Meanwhile, prepare the sauce. Put a tablespoon of oil, the chopped onion and lard into a pan and sauté over a medium heat. Add the minced meat, the chopped parsley and rosemary and continue to sauté. Blend in the tomato, a ladleful of water and cook slowly for about one hour, adding more water, if necessary. Cook the pasta in abundant salted water, drain and dress with the sauce and grated Pecorino. Serve hot.

Did you know that…
This is a typical Sardinian pasta and it can be accompanied by any type of sauce, thanks to its shape and because it is made out of only durum wheat flour and water. In Sardinia it is known by the name of "aidos cicones" or "maccarones aravaos."

Malloreddus al tonno con bottarga di muggine
Malloreddus (Sardinian pasta) with tuna and gray mullet roe

Servings 4
Difficulty *Medium*
Region *Sardinia*

Fish

14 oz (400 g) malloreddus typical Sardinian pasta – 7 oz (200 g) tuna, fresh – 4¼ oz (120 g) onion – 3⅜ tablespoons (5 cl) extra virgin olive oil – ½ oz (15 g) capers – 3½ oz (100 g) fresh tomatoes – 1 oz (30 g) wild fennel – ½ cup (10 cl) white wine – ¾ oz (20 g) gray mullet roe (bottarga di muggine) – ½ cup (10 cl) fish broth (optional) – salt and pepper.

25 minutes preparation time + 5 minutes cooking time

Cut the onion finely and dice the tuna. Put the oil in a large pan with the onion over a medium heat. Add the tuna and gently fry for 2 minutes. Add the capers. Pour the white wine over it and allow to evaporate. Season with salt and pepper. If necessary pour a little of the fish stock on the tuna. Add the roughly chopped tomatoes and half of the fennel.

If the sauce is too dry, add a little of the fish stock.

Cook the pasta in salted boiling water and drain when it is cooked "al dente." Pour on the sauce and add the wild fennel. Sprinkle the grated fish roe over the dish.

Chef's Tips
The bottarga is always added at the end of cooking, well away from the heat, to avoid losing its taste.

Maltagliati con i porri
Maltagliati with leek sauce

Servings 4
Difficulty *Low*
Region *Piedmont*

Vegetable

14⅛ oz (400 g) all-purpose flour – 4 eggs – 4 leeks – 2⅛ oz (60 g) butter – ⅞ cup (2 dl) single cream – 2¾ oz (80 g) grated Parmigiano Reggiano cheese – salt to taste.

30 minutes preparation time + 15 minutes cooking time

Put the flour on a work surface and make a well. Add the eggs and mix to make a uniform dough. Leave the dough to rest and cover with a cloth or plastic wrap. Roll out the dough with a machine to a thickness of about 0.05 inches (1.5 mm), leave to dry and cut into diamond shapes, with sides approximately 1⅓ inches (3 cm) long.
Clean and wash the leeks and cut into thin slices.
Over a medium heat gently fry the leeks in the butter.
Cook the pasta in plenty of boiling salted water and when it is cooked drain and add it to the leeks in the pan. Add the cream, mix well and finish with a sprinkling of grated Parmesan cheese.
Serve hot.

Orecchiette con broccoli, pomodorini e mandorle
Pasta with broccoli, tomatoes and almonds

Servings 4
Difficulty Low
Region Apulia

Fish

14⅛ oz (400 g) orecchiette – 12⅓ oz (350 g) broccoli – 2¾ oz (80 g) Pecorino cheese – ¾ oz (20 g) salted anchovies – 1 clove of garlic – 2 tablespoons (30 g) extra virgin olive oil – 7 oz (200 g) cherry tomatoes – salt – black pepper – 1 oz (30 g) almonds, sliced.

20 minutes preparation time + 15 minutes cooking time

Crush the garlic, fillet and break up the anchovies.

Wash the broccoli, remove the florets and blanch for 3 minutes. Cut the cherry tomatoes in half. Sauté the garlic and anchovies over a medium heat.

Add the broccoli, then the tomato, and leave to cook over a low heat for 5 minutes. Season with salt and pepper and add a little oil.

In a casserole containing boiling salted water, cook the "orecchiette" and drain when they are cooked "al dente." Mix in the sauce.

Serve the "orecchiette" and decorate with slivers of Pecorino and flaked almonds.

Did you know that...
The broccoli must be cooked in boiling salted water because in this way it maintains its green color and the heads do not break up. Because of their shape, the "orecchiette" tend to clump together during cooking; it is a good idea to stir them continuously during the first few minutes of cooking.

Chef's Tips
This is a typical hard wheat pasta dish from the Puglia region. It is known as "strascinati" (lit. "dragged out"), and is accompanied by rather thin sauces, since it absorbs a lot of liquid.

Passatelli con prosciutto, rucola, pomodorini e melanzane
Passatelli pasta with prosciutto, arugula, cherry tomatoes and eggplants

Servings 4
Difficulty *Medium*
Region *Emilia Romagna*

Meat

For the passatelli pasta: 10½ oz (300 g) breadcrumbs – 7 oz (200 g) grated Parmigiano Reggiano cheese – 2½ oz (70 g) Parma ham – 1 oz (30 g) all-purpose flour – 4 eggs.
For the Sauce: 3 bunches arugula – 1 eggplant, medium sized – 3½ oz (100 g) cherry tomatoes – 1¾ oz (30 g) almonds – 2¾ oz (80 g) Parmigiano Reggiano cheese, in slivers – 1⅓ tablespoons (2 cl) Extra Virgin Olive Oil – 1 clove of garlic.

15 minutes preparation time + 15 minutes cooking time

Finely mince the ham in order to avoid the meat from sticking in the holes of the utensil for making the passatelli.

Add the minced ham to the other ingredients for the passatelli, and mix them together.

Then form the mixture into balls, wrap them in plastic wrap and leave in the fridge for about an hour.

Clean the vegetables, cut the tomatoes and remove the seeds. Cut the eggplant into small cubes and sauté in a pan with olive oil. Put the arugula, the almonds, the parmigiano, the garlic and the extra virgin olive oil in a blender. Blend until you obtain a creamy consistency.

Mix the cherry tomatoes with the eggplant and cook the passatelli in salted water or broth. Drain and toss in a pan with the vegetables and the arugula pesto. Put into dishes and serve.

Penne lisce alle melanzane e pesce spada
Smooth penne with eggplant and swordfish

Servings 4
Difficulty *Low*
Region *Sicily*

Fish

14⅛ oz (400 g) smooth penne – ⅔ cup (15 dl) extra virgin olive oil – 7 oz (200 g) eggplant – 7 oz (200 g) swordfish – 8 basil leaves – 5⅓ oz (150 g) cherry tomatoes – ⅓ cup (8 cl) white wine – 5⅓ oz (150 g) salted ricotta – 1 clove of garlic – salt – pepper.

20 minutes preparation time + 20 minutes cooking time

Wash the eggplants and dice them. Heat ½ cup (1 dl) of oil over a high heat and when it is hot, fry the eggplants. As soon as they are golden, remove them from the oil using a skimmer, dry them on absorbent paper and keep them warm. Cut the swordfish into cubes. In a large pan, heat the rest of the oil over a medium heat and when it is hot, add the crushed garlic, the swordfish and fry gently for a few minutes. Wash the tomatoes, cut them into segments and add them to the fish in the pan. Stir the contents of the pan, pour the white wine over it and simmer until it evaporates. Add the basil leaves cut into bits roughly by hand and salt and pepper to taste. Cook the pasta in abundant boiling salted water and strain it when it is cooked "al dente." Add the sauce prepared as above, together with the fried eggplant, the grated ricotta and serve.

Chef's Tips
The cubes of eggplant must be fried in very hot oil so as to immediately form a crust, and prevent them from absorbing the oil.

Pizzoccheri
Pizzoccheri

Servings 4
Difficulty **Medium**
Region **Lombardy**

Vegetable

For the pasta: 8¾ oz (250 g) buckwheat flour, black – 2⅓ oz (75 g) all-purpose flour – ¾ cup (16.5 cc) water.
For the sauce: 12⅓ oz (350 g) cabbages, white – 8¾ oz (250 g) butter – 8¾ oz (250 g) Casera cheese – 2 cloves of garlic – 3½ oz (100 g) grated Parmigiano Reggiano cheese – salt.

30 minutes preparation time + 15 minutes cooking time

Mix the two types of flour, the black and the white on a work surface, add the water and make into a dough. Knead for at least fifteen minutes until velvety. Then roll out the dough into a layer less than 0.2 inches (½ cm) thick and cut it into strips about 2.8 inches (7 cm) long.

Place the strips one on top of the other and cut them crosswise into tagliatelle just over 0.2 inch (0.5 cm) wide. Cut the Casera cheese into very thin slices and keep in the fridge. Fill a large pot with water and bring to the boil then drop in the cabbage leaves torn into chunks with your hands (or the chard stems cut into pieces about 2 inches (5 cm) long).

After five minutes add some coarse salt to the water and drop in the "pizzoccheri" which must cook in vigorously boiling water for 7-10 minutes. Before draining, taste the pizzoccheri to make sure they are tender but not overcooked. Also taste the greens to make sure they have the right texture.

Then, using a slotted spoon, take out of the pot some pizzoccheri and greens, put into an oval serving dish and sprinkle with grated Parmesan cheese and thin slices of caséra cheese. Continue until all the pizzoccheri and greens are drained and dressed.

Finally drizzle over some butter melted with a garlic clove. Serve on hot plates.

The quantities of butter may seem excessive; in the traditional recipe, the pizzoccheri are immersed in melted butter in the serving dishes.

Quadrucci con le fave
Pasta with broad beans

Servings 4
Difficulty Low
Region Latium

Meat

1 ¾ lb (800 g) fresh small broad beans – 10½ oz (300 g) flour – 3 eggs – 1 onion –
6 mint leaves – 10½ oz (300 g) canned peeled tomatoes – 3½ oz (100 g) ham – 1½
tablespoons (2 cl) extra virgin olive oil – salt – pepper.

40 minutes preparation time + 1 hour cooking time

Prepare the fresh pasta by mixing the flour with the eggs to obtain a smooth dough. Leave it to rest for 20 minutes.

Roll out the pasta into thin sheets and cut it into strips about ¾ inch (2 cm) wide and then cut it again to make squares. Leave the pasta to dry on a floured chopping board. Chop up the ham fat, the mint and the onion.

Heat the oil in a large pan over a medium heat, add the chopped ingredients and sauté for about 5 minutes. Add the diced ham, a glass of water, the drained tomatoes, and the shelled beans which preferably should be small (to shell the beans blanch them in boiling water for 1 minute).

Cook over a low heat for about 1 hour adding water, if necessary. Season with salt and pepper. When the beans are cooked, add the "quadrucci." Serve hot.

Schiaffoni al guanciale
Pasta with bacon sauce

Servings 4
Difficulty *Low*
Region *Basilicata*

Meat

14 ⅛ oz (400 g) pasta (schiaffoni) – 5 ⅓ oz (150 g) pork cheek – 1 clove of garlic –
1 ⅓ tablespoons (2 cl) extra virgin olive oil – 1 tablespoon parsley, chopped – salt
and pepper – 1 ¾ oz (50 g) Pecorino cheese, grated – ½ cup (1 dl) dry white wine
– paprika (optional) – pepper.

10 minutes preparation time + 10 minutes cooking time

Gently fry two thirds of the pounded pork cheek and the garlic and when the pork cheek is golden, add the wine and simmer until it reduces. Add the rest of the diced bacon to the pan. Cook the pasta in salted boiling water and drain when it is cooked "al dente." Mix in the sauce, add the chopped parsley, grated Pecorino, a pinch of pepper, the paprika, season with salt and serve.

Agnolotti di Pontebba
Agnolotti with a sweet filling

Servings 4
*Difficulty **Medium***
*Region **Friuli**
Venezia Giulia*

Vegetable

For the pasta: ½ lb (250 g) all-purpose flour – 1 egg – salt – water.
For the filling: ½ lb (250 g) ricotta cheese – 3 ½ oz (100 g) prunes – 1 dried fig – 1 full tablespoon sugar – salt.
For the sauce: cinnamon – ¾ oz (20 g) sugar – 3 ½ oz (100 g) butter.

30 minutes preparation time + 10 minutes cooking time

Put the flour on a pastry board and make a well in it, add the eggs and mix to make a smooth dough. Leave to rest for 20 minutes.

Roll out the pasta in thin sheets with the help of a machine. Cut out disks 1 ½-2 inches (4-5 cm) in diameter, then in the center of each disk put a little of the filling made mixing together the dry figs and prunes boiled in water, chopped and mixed with ricotta cheese and sugar.

Close the discs in half-moon or crescent shapes, being careful to seal the edges well and then drop them into salted boiling water for 5 minutes. Drain and add melted butter, sugar and cinnamon.

Regional name: Cjalzòns di Ponteibe

166

Angiulottos
Sardinian ravioli

Servings 4
Difficulty Medium
Region Sardinia

Varie versioni

Meat version: 1 lb (400 g) ground meat – 4 eggs – 5 ⅓ oz (150 g) Pecorino cheese – salt – pepper.
Cheese version: 1 lb 1 ½ oz (500 g) Pecorino cheese, fresh – 4 eggs – salt – pepper.
Ricotta version: 3 ½ oz (100 g) ricotta – 4 eggs – 1 lb (400 g) grated Pecorino cheese.
For pasta: ½ lb (250 g) durum wheat flour – 1 tablespoon (1 cl) extra virgin olive oil – sachet of saffron – salt and pepper.
For the sauce: 4 ¼ oz (120 g) butter – 3 ½ oz (100 g) Pecorino cheese.

40 minutes preparation time + 5 minutes cooking time

Put the flour on a pastry board and make a well in it, add water, oil, salt, saffron and mix to make a smooth dough. Leave to rest for 20 minutes.

Meanwhile prepare the filling, which can be of three types: with meat ("Angiulottos de Pezza"), cheese ("Angiulottos de Casu") or Ricotta ("Angiulottos de Arrescottu").

For the meat filling, take the minced meat, gently fry it in oil then mix it with grated Pecorino and 4 eggs, pepper and a pinch of salt. The stuffing is ready to fill the "angiulottos."

For the cheese filling, chop up some fresh Pecorino and mix with an egg, pepper and salt to taste and a pinch of saffron. For the Ricotta filling, proceed in the same way as for the cheese filling.

Roll the pasta into thin sheets with a machine. Cut into squares with 2 inch (5 cm) sides and fill with the filling prepared beforehand. Cook in abundant boiling salted water, drain and dress with butter and grated Pecorino cheese before serving.

Cappellacci di zucca
Pumpkin ravioli

Servings 4
Difficulty *Medium*
Region *Emilia Romagna*

Vegetable

For the pasta: 10½ oz (300 g) flour – 3 eggs.
For the filling: 2¼ lb (1 kg) yellow pumpkins – 7 oz (200 g) grated Parmesan cheese – nutmeg – 1 egg – salt.

40 minutes preparation time + 5 minutes cooking time

Make a well in the flour and add the eggs. Mix until you obtain a smooth dough. Leave to rest for about 20 minutes. Slice the pumpkin and cook in a hot oven, in plenty of salted boiling water or steam after having removed the seeds and the strings. Remove the skin, sieve and dry with a cloth to remove the excess liquid. Mix in the Parmesan cheese, the egg and season with salt and nutmeg.
Leave the filling to rest for about half an hour.
Roll out the pasta into a thin sheet and cut it into 2 inch (6 cm) squares. In the center of each square put a small amount of the filling, the size of a small walnut. Fold it in half into a triangle, and press the edges together with your fingers to make sure that the filling does not come out during cooking. Bring the two far corners together and press with your fingers. Cook the pasta in abundant salted boiling water, drain when it is cooked "al dente" and dress with melted butter and grated Parmesan cheese. This pasta can also be served with a bolognese meat sauce.

Did you know that…
The name of this pasta comes from the shape of the straw hats typically worn by country folk. Indeed, its origins date back to the times of the Este court, famous for its refined cuisine: the steward and master of ceremonies, Giovan Battista Rossetti mentioned it in his recipe book in 1584.

Cappelletti in brodo
Cappelletti in broth

Servings 4
Difficulty *Medium*
Region *Emilia Romagna*

Meat

14 oz (400 g) all-purpose flour – 10½ oz (300 g) Parmigiano Reggiano cheese: – 7 oz (200 g) lean pork – 7 oz (200 g) ham – 3½ oz (100 g) chicken breast – broth – 2 oz (50 g) butter – 5 eggs – olive oil – pepper – nutmeg – salt.

1 h preparation time + 10 minutes cooking time

In a pan, melt the butter over a medium heat then add finely ground pork and chicken breast. Cook for about 15 minutes, then add chopped ham and continue cooking for a couple of minutes. Then remove from the heat and leave to cool. Mince all the meat finely in a mincer and add the Parmesan cheese and an egg.

Mix until soft and smooth. Add a pinch of salt and nutmeg. This is the classic filling, but there are many variations: you can use Mortadella instead of ham, roast veal instead of pork, or turkey breast in addition to the pork or hen fat (or even better capon fat) instead of butter. One of the many variations calls for a filling made entirely from stewed meat with cloves and onion.

Prepare the pasta dough using the eggs, flour, salt and olive oil. Let it rest under a kitchen towel for about 30 minutes. Then roll out into a thin sheet.

Cut the sheet of dough into horizontal strips and then cut vertically, so that you have 1½ in (3-4 cm) squares. Place a tiny amount of filling at the center of each square and fold into a triangle, sealing the edges. (If the pasta is too dry, brush the edges with a drop of water.)

Squeeze together your thumb and index finger of both hands on either end of the triangle, so that the point is facing upwards. Rotate the cappelletti to the right towards your left index finger and place the corners on top of one another until they are united.

The cappelletti must be left to rest for several hours to harden. Cook in capon broth for ten minutes. Serve with plenty of broth and a sprinkling of Parmesan cheese.

Lasagne alla napoletana
Neapolitan-style lasagne

Servings 4
Difficulty *Medium*
Region *Campania*

Meat

For the pasta: 10½ oz (300 g) all-purpose flour – 3 eggs – 2 teaspoons (1 cl) extra virgin olive oil – salt to taste.
For the filling: 5⅓ oz (150 g) pork sausage, sautéed – 9 oz (250 g) ricotta cheese – 2 eggs, hard-boiled – 3½ oz (100 g) mozzarella cheese – 2 oz (60 g) grated Parmigiano Reggiano cheese – 1 small carrot – 1 stalk of celery – 1 small onion – 1 sprig of marjoram – 1¾ oz (50 g) lardo (fat bacon) – 10½ oz (300 g) minced beef – ⅔ cup (1.5 dl) red wine – ¼ cup (5 cl) extra virgin olive oil – ⅓ oz (10 g) flour – 9 oz (250 g) tomatoes, (pulp).

1 hour preparation time+ 40 minutes cooking time

Cook the eggs in salted water for 10 minutes.

In a small casserole, gently fry the chopped lardo with the oil and the chopped vegetables. Add the minced meat and sauté. Pour the wine over it, sprinkle with the marjoram and season with salt and pepper. When the wine has evaporated, mix in a small amount of flour and leave to cook for a few minutes. Then add the tomatoes and leave to cook for about 1 hour, if necessary thinning with a little stock. Put the flour on a work-surface and make a well in it. Put the eggs and the oil in the well. Mix to make a uniform smooth dough. Leave to rest for 20 minutes and then roll the dough out into a thin sheet with a machine. Then cut it into strips the length of the oven dish you will be using. Parboil the pasta in plenty of salted water for 40 seconds. Drain and leave to dry on a cloth.

In a buttered oven dish, arrange the pasta in layers, putting the meat sauce between each layer.

On top of the sauce, uniformly distribute the sausage cut into in small pieces, touches of the ricotta, the hard-boiled eggs in wedges or slices and the mozzarella in cubes.

Finish with a sheet of pasta and sprinkle grated Parmesan on top. Cook in a moderate oven at 350°F (180°C) for around 30 minutes. Once it is cooked, well-browned on the surface, leave it to rest before serving.

Lasagne verdi alla bolognese
Green lasagna Bolognese

Servings 4
Difficulty **Medium**
Region **Emilia Romagna**

Meat

For the sauce: ½ onion, sliced – 1 carrot, grated – 1 stalk of celery, chopped – 1 oz (30 g) butter – 7 oz (200 g) minced beef – 5¼ (150 g) minced pork – 2 oz (60 g) tomato paste – ½ cup (1 dl) red wine – salt – pepper.
For the pasta: 10½ oz (300 g) all-purpose flour – 2 eggs – 5¼ (150 g) spinach.
For the bechamel sauce: 4¼₄ pints (2 l) of milk – 5⅔ oz (160 g) butter – 5⅔ oz (160 g) flour – 7 oz (200 g) Parmigiano Reggiano cheese, grated.

2 hours preparation time + 30 minutes cooking time

Put the oil and vegetables in pan and soften over a medium heat.

Add the meat and turn up the heat so it fries gently. Add the red wine and cook until it evaporates completely. Lower the heat and add the tomato paste. Season with salt and pepper and add the water. Simmer for about 30 minutes.

Put the flour on a work surface and make a well. Put the eggs and the spinach, which has already been blanched, drained and chopped, in the well. Mix to obtain a smooth uniform dough. Leave to rest for 20 minutes and roll into thin sheets using a machine. Cut into strips the length of the oven dish you will be using.

Parboil the pasta in plenty of salted water for 20 seconds. Drain and dry on a cloth

In a small pan melt the butter and add the flour. Then add the hot milk little by little and bring to the boil. Add salt and when the liquid thickens the bechamel sauce is ready.

In a greased oven dish put a layer of meat sauce, cover with grated Parmesan cheese with a sheet of pasta on top. Then a layer of sauce, a layer of bechamel with cheese and then another sheet of pasta and so on until there are about 4 or 5 layers.

Cover with bechamel and dot with butter. Cook in a medium oven at 350°F (180°C) for about 30 minutes until the top is golden. Leave for 15 minutes before serving.

Ravioli del Pim con caprino erbette e pesto leggero
"Pim" ravioli with goat cheese, herbs and light pesto

Servings 4
*Difficulty **Medium***

Vegetable

For the pasta and the filling: 10½ oz (300 g) all-purpose flour – 3 eggs – ¼ cup (60 g) extra virgin olive oil – salt to taste – water – 5⅓ oz (150 g) goat cheese – 2¾ oz (80 g) ricotta cheese – 2¾ oz (80 g) Parmigiano Reggiano cheese – 1 pinch (1 g) marjoram, fresh – 1 pinch (1 g) thyme, fresh – 2 leaves of basil – 1 egg, whole fresh – salt and pepper to taste – 1 bay leaf.

For the light pesto sauce: 2¾ tablespoons (4 cl) extra virgin olive oil – 1 oz (30 g) basil – ¾ oz (20 g) pine nuts – 1½ oz (40 g) Parmigiano Reggiano cheese – ¾ oz (20 g) Pecorino cheese.

40 minutes preparation time + 5 minutes cooking time

Sieve the ricotta and goat's milk cheese.

Add the chopped aromatic herbs, the egg and the Parmesan cheese. Season with salt and pepper and mix together well.

Put the flour on a work surface and make a well, break the eggs into the well and mix to make a uniform dough. Wrap the pasta dough in plastic wrap and put in the fridge for 30 minutes. Roll out the dough into very thin sheets with a machine, lay on a table and put a small quantity of the filling in the center of the pasta.

After filling, lay the another sheet of pasta on top, making sure the edges are well-sealed. Make the ravioli by cutting them out with a ravioli pasta cutter.

Prepare the pesto by blending the ingredients listed in a blender.

Meanwhile, cook the ravioli in abundant boiling salted water. Once they are cooked, drain and arrange on a plate. Add a little of the cooking liquid to the pesto and pour onto the ravioli. Decorate the plate with drops of pesto and small aromatic herb leaves.

Tortelli di erbette
Tortelli filled with Swiss chard and ricotta

Servings 4
Difficulty Medium
Region Emilia Romagna

Vegetable

For pasta: 10½ oz (300 g) "00" flour – 3 eggs.
For the filling: 1 bunch Swiss chard – 1½ lb (700 g) full-fat ricotta cheese – 1¾ oz (50 g) Parmigiano Reggiano cheese, grated – 1 oz (30 g) butter – 1 egg – ground nutmeg – salt.
For the sauce: 2⅛ oz (60 g) butter – 2⅛ oz (60 g) Parmigiano Reggiano cheese, grated.

1 hour preparation time + 5 minutes cooking time

Put the flour on a work surface and make a well, add the eggs and mix to make a smooth dough. Leave to rest for 20 minutes.

Bring a large pan of water to the boil and cook the Swiss chard. Drain and squeeze all the water out. Sieve the ricotta and add the Parmesan, the softened butter, the egg, the chopped Swiss chard and season with salt and nutmeg.

Roll out the pasta into thin sheets and cut out 3 inch (8 cm) squares. Place small portions of the filling, the size of a walnut, on top of the pasta. Then fold the square of pasta to form a triangle and press down on the edges with a fork to seal them. Cook the tortelli in abundant salted boiling water. Drain when they are cooked "al dente" and pour on the melted butter, sprinkle with Parmigiano and serve.

Tortelli di ricotta e salvia
Ricotta and sage tortelli

Servings 4
Difficulty Medium
Region Emilia Romagna

Vegetable

For the pasta: 14⅛ oz (400 g) flour – 3 eggs – 3½ tablespoons (5 cl) dry white wine – salt.
For the filling: 1 tablespoon parsley, chopped – 1¾ oz (50 g) grated Parmesan cheese – 1 lb 1⅝ oz (500 g) ricotta cheese – 1 egg – nutmeg – salt – white pepper.
For the sauce: 8 sage leaves – 3½ oz (100 g) heavy cream – ¾ oz (20 g) butter – 1¾ oz (50 g) grated Parmesan cheese.
1 hour preparation time + 5 minutes cooking time

Prepare the tortelli filling by mixing the all the ingredients thoroughly and then leave to rest.
Then prepare the pasta dough, mix together the flour with the eggs, the wine and the salt. Then cover and leave to rest for at least 10 minutes.
For the sauce: melt the butter with the sage in a large pan over a low heat and when it is hot add the cream and cook for about 3 minutes. Meanwhile, make the tortelli: roll out the pasta into thin sheets and cut out 2 inch (5 cm) squares. Place a walnut-size amount of the filling in the center and close with another square, sealing the edges well to avoid them opening during cooking.
Cook the tortelli in abundant salted water, drain and empty into the sauce. Toss over a medium heat and add the grated Parmesan cheese.
Divide the pasta between heated individual plates and serve immediately.

Vincisgrassi alla marchigiana
"Vincisgrassi" from the Marches

Servings 4
Difficulty Medium
Region Marches

Meat

For the sauce: 2¾ oz (80 g) butter – 1¾ oz (50 g) all-purpose flour – 5⅓ oz (150 g) cooked ham – 3½ oz (100 g) lean minced meat – 1¾ oz (50 g) Acqualagna truffle – 1¼ cups (3 dl) cream – 4¼ cups (1 l) milk – salt and pepper to taste.
For the crepes: 1½ oz (40 g) all-purpose flour – 5 oz eggs – ½ oz extra virgin olive oil – ½ cup milk – ¾ oz cooked wine – 1½ oz Parmigiano Reggiano cheese – salt to taste.

1 hour preparation time + 45 minutes cooking time

Put the oil and the Parmigiano cheese to one side, mix the rest of the ingredients for the crepes to obtain a smooth mixture. Place a pan on a medium flame, smear the surface with butter and cook the crepes, using up all the mixture.

In a casserole over a medium flame, fry the diced ham together with the minced meat for 10 minutes. Add the flour and let it dry up and become slightly crisp. Add the milk and let it cook for at least 30 minutes. Season with salt and pepper to taste.

Thicken with the cream and flavor with the finely sliced truffle. In a greased oven dish alternate a layer of crepes with a layer of the sauce until all the ingredients are used, so that there is a layer of sauce on top. Sprinkle with the Parmesan cheese and bake at 350°F (180°C) until the surface is golden brown.

Remove from the oven and allow to cool slightly before serving the portions.

Bomba di riso
Rice bomb

Servings 4
Difficulty **Medium**
Region **Tuscany**

Meat

12½ oz (350 g) rice – 2 tablespoons extra virgin olive oil – ¾ oz (20 g) butter – 1 small onion, finely chopped – 7 oz (200 g) veal – 1¾ oz (50 g) calf sweetbread – 1¾ oz (50 g) pork sausage – 1 small stalk celery – 1 small carrot, chopped – 1 pinch cinnamon powder – 7 oz (200 g) canned tomatoes, without juice and seeds – 2 ladles broth – juice of 1 lemon – 2 eggs – 1 oz (30 g) grated Parmigiano Reggiano cheese – 4 capers, chopped – 1¾ oz (50 g) breadcrumbs.

1 hour preparation time – 5 minutes cooking time

Cook the rice in boiling, salted water, and when it is half cooked, drain it and allow it to cool. In a pan, mix together the extra-virgin olive oil and butter and sauté a finely chopped onion well.

Add the veal, sausage and diced sweetbreads, a stick of celery and a chopped carrot. Cook until golden and add a pinch of cinnamon and the peeled, seeded tomatoes, without their juice. Pour over two ladles of stock, cook for 40 minutes over a low heat, put the already cooled rice in a large bowl and add the juice of a lemon, the whole eggs, the grated Parmesan cheese, chopped capers and a part of the sauce and mix well.

Grease the pudding mold with butter, sprinkle with bread crumbs and pour in the rice, leaving aside at least a fifth. Make a deep hollow in the center, pour in the meat and cover with the remaining rice. Dust with bread crumbs and small flakes of butter.

Bake in a pre-heated oven at 390°F (200°C) for about 20 minutes.

Bomba di riso
Rice bomb

Servings 4
Difficulty **Medium**
Region **Tuscany**

Meat

12½ oz (350 g) rice – 2 tablespoons extra virgin olive oil – ¾ oz (20 g) butter – 1 small onion, finely chopped – 7 oz (200 g) veal – 1¾ oz (50 g) calf sweetbread – 1¾ oz (50 g) pork sausage – 1 small stalk celery – 1 small carrot, chopped – 1 pinch cinnamon powder – 7 oz (200 g) canned tomatoes, without juice and seeds – 2 ladles broth – juice of 1 lemon – 2 eggs – 1 oz (30 g) grated Parmigiano Reggiano cheese – 4 capers, chopped – 1¾ oz (50 g) breadcrumbs.

1 hour preparation time – 5 minutes cooking time

Cook the rice in boiling, salted water, and when it is half cooked, drain it and allow it to cool. In a pan, mix together the extra-virgin olive oil and butter and sauté a finely chopped onion well.

Add the veal, sausage and diced sweetbreads, a stick of celery and a chopped carrot. Cook until golden and add a pinch of cinnamon and the peeled, seeded tomatoes, without their juice. Pour over two ladles of stock, cook for 40 minutes over a low heat, put the already cooled rice in a large bowl and add the juice of a lemon, the whole eggs, the grated Parmesan cheese, chopped capers and a part of the sauce and mix well.

Grease the pudding mold with butter, sprinkle with bread crumbs and pour in the rice, leaving aside at least a fifth. Make a deep hollow in the center, pour in the meat and cover with the remaining rice. Dust with bread crumbs and small flakes of butter.

Bake in a pre-heated oven at 390°F (200°C) for about 20 minutes.

Risotto agli asparagi
Risotto with asparagus

Servings 4
Difficulty **Medium**
Region **Lombardy**

Vegetable

2¼ lb (1 kg) asparagus – 1 lb 1⅝ oz (500 g) rice – 5⅓ oz (150 g) Taleggio cheese, or similar cheese – 4¼ oz (120 g) butter – 1 small onion – salt.

15 minutes preparation + 20 minutes cooking time

Wash the asparagus thoroughly under running water, remove the white part. Cut the asparagus into disks and put the tips to one side. Put the asparagus in boiling water and drain when it is cooked "al dente." Keep the cooking water for cooking the rice.

Toast the rice and then add the cooking water from the asparagus, a little at a time. When the rice is cooked, add the asparagus, the butter, the onion and the diced cheese. Season with salt and pepper. Stir well and serve.

Did you know that…
It is traditional in Lombardy to use grated Parmesan cheese.

Risotto al Barbera
Risotto with Barbera wine

Servings 4
Difficulty Medium
Region Piedmont

Meat

13 oz (360 g) rice – meat broth – 2 onions – 1¾ oz (50g) beef bone marrow – 3 cups Barbera wine – 3 tablespoons tomato sauce – 2¾ oz (80 g) butter – 2¾ oz (80 g) grated Parmesan cheese – tablespoon extra virgin olive oil – 2 bay leaves – 1 small bunch sage – black pepper, freshly ground – nutmeg.

10 minutes preparation time + 20 minutes cooking time

Finely slice the onions and sauté them in a saucepan with oil, ¾ oz (20 g) butter, the ground beef marrow and bay leaves. When the onions are soft, add half the wine to the sautéed onions and reduce. Add rice (Baldo rice or Roma rice) turn up the heat and stir with a wooden spoon until the ingredients are thoroughly mixed.

As soon as the rice is toasted, add the rest of the wine which has been diluted with a ladle of broth, two tablespoons of tomato purée and the sage leaves, which will be removed before serving. Once this wine has also been absorbed, allow the rice to cook, gradually adding beef broth.

Stir in the remaining butter and the cheese, sprinkle generously with freshly ground black pepper and freshly ground nutmeg and add 3-4 tablespoons of hot Barbera wine.

This risotto used to be eaten with a spoon, never with a fork.

Risotto alla milanese
Milanese-style risotto

Servings 4
Difficulty Medium
Region Lombardy

Meat

11 ¼ (320 g) Superfino rice – 1 ¾ oz (50 g) beef bone marrow – 2 ¾ oz (80 g) butter – 1 ¾ oz (50 g) onion – ½ cup (1 dl) white wine – 4 ¼ cups (1 l) meat broth – 1 packet saffron – 2 ⅛ oz (60 g) grated Parmigiano Reggiano cheese – 1 ¾ oz (50 g) veal extract (fondo bruno) – salt and pepper to taste – ¼ oz saffron pistils – 1 ¾ oz (50 g) extra virgin olive oil.

30 minutes preparation time + 20 minutes cooking time

Over a medium heat soften the onion in half the butter. Stir in the rice and fry gently for a minute.

Pour the white wine over it, allow to evaporate, and add the previously crumbled marrow. Cover the rice with boiling meat stock and continue cooking. Five minutes before the rice has finished cooking, add the saffron and season.

When all the liquid has been absorbed by the rice, but when it is still "al dente," remove from the heat. Whisk in the remaining butter and Parmesan cheese.

Did you know that…
This is the dish that symbolizes Lombardy, the simplicity of the rice is enhanced by the flavor and the color of saffron.

Chef's Tips
It can be served as a first course or as a side dish accompanying veal dishes; above all the Milanese "Ossobuco."

Risotto di scampi e fiori di zucca
Risotto with scampi and zucchini flowers

Servings 4
Difficulty Medium
Region Marches

Fish

10½ oz (300 g) rice – 16 zucchini flowers – 14⅛ oz (400 g) scampi – 6⅓ cups (1.5 l) fish broth – ½ onion – extra virgin olive oil – ¾ oz (20 g) butter – salt – 3½ tablespoons (5 cl) white wine.

20 minutes preparation time + 20 minutes cooking time

Pour a little oil into a large saucepan and place over heat. Then add the finely chopped onion and sauté over a low heat for a couple of minutes without allowing the onion to brown. Then add the rice and toast over medium heat for a couple of minutes, stirring continuously. The rice must be thoroughly toasted so that it gives the right flavor to the risotto. Then add the white wine.

Once the wine has evaporated, begin cooking the rice over a high flame, adding a ladle of boiling stock at a time and stirring occasionally so that the rice does not stick to the bottom of the pot. Then add the zucchini flowers, and lastly the scampi. When the rice is almost cooked, season with salt and stir in a knob of butter. Continue to cook, adding the remaining stock a little at a time.

Did you know that...
Rice was brought to Italy by the Arabs in the 9th century when they occupied Sicily, and where it is still much used in traditional recipes like arancini *(or fried rice balls). Rice, however, became even more popular in northern Italy, especially in Lombardy and Piedmont, the home of risotto.*

Chef's Tips
Rice continues to cook for a couple of minutes even after being removed from the heat. In order not to overcook it, turn off the heat with the rice is still slightly "al dente."

Risotto Giuseppe Verdi
Risotto Giuseppe Verdi

Servings 4
Difficulty **Medium**
Region **Emilia Romagna**

Meat

13⅓ oz (350 g) Carnaroli rice – 3½ oz (100 g) butter – 2¾ oz (80 g) mushrooms – 2¾ oz (80 g) asparagus tips – 2¾ oz (80 g) Parma ham – 2¾ oz (80 g) peeled tomatoes – ¼ cup (5cl) single cream – 4¼ cups (1 l) meat broth – 2¾ oz (80 g) grated Parmigiano Reggiano cheese – ½ onion, thinly sliced.

25 minutes preparation time + 20 minutes cooking time

Clean and chop the onion. Wash the mushrooms and cut into thin slices.
Clean the asparagus and boil. Keep only the tips. Cut the ham à la julienne and dice the tomatoes.
In a saucepan, sauté the onion in butter. Add the rice and gently fry for a minute. Add the mushrooms, ham, the asparagus, the prosciutto and the diced tomatoes. Add the stock, little by little and when it is half cooked, add the cream.
When it is cooked "al dente" mix in the rest of the butter and the Parmesan cheese.

Zuppetta di Cogne
Rice soup from Cogne

Servings 4
Difficulty Medium
Region Valle d'Aosta

Vegetable

11 ¼ oz (320 g) rice – 1 lb 1 ⅝ oz (500 g) bread – 7 oz (200 g) Fontina cheese – 5 ⅓ oz (150 g) butter – 8 ½ cups (2 l) meat broth – salt.

10 minutes preparation time + 30 minutes cooking time

Cut the Fontina into slices. Slice the bread and fry in 1 ¾ oz (50 g) of the butter. In another pan sauté the rice in 1 ¾ oz (50 g) butter over a medium heat for 2 minutes. Add the boiling stock, a little at a time and continue to cook for about 12 minutes. In a large oven dish, arrange one layer of bread, one of risotto and one of Fontina, continuing in alternate layers and finishing off with one of Fontina. Add a little stock to soften the ingredients, melt the rest of the butter and pour it over the dish. Cook in a moderate oven 350°F (180°C) for about 10 minutes.

Anolini
Anolini

Servings 4
Difficulty Medium
Region Emilia Romagna

Meat

For pasta: 1 lb (400 g) all-purpose flour – 2 eggs – ½ cup (120 g) water.
For the filling: 10½ oz (300 g) leg of beef – 2½ oz (75 g) butter – 5 oz (150 g) bread-crumbs – 5 oz (150 g) grated Parmigiano Reggiano cheese – 1 stalk celery – 1 carrot – 1 onion – 1 clove – 1 teaspoon tomato paste – 2 eggs – salt and pepper – nutmeg – 1 cup (2 dl) red wine – 9 cups (2 l) meat broth.

10 h cooking time for the braised meat – 1 hour preparation time – 5 minutes cooking time

Melt the butter in a pot, preferably earthenware, and then add chopped vegetables and fry gently. Then add the meat and clove.

Once the meat begins to brown, cover with red wine and a little warm water. Cook over a very low heat for about 10 hours, adding the tomato paste halfway through cooking.

By the time it is cooked, the meat will have dissolved into a dense sauce. Mix in the breadcrumbs.

Then add the grated Parmigiano Reggiano and if desired the liquidized vegetables from the broth. Add the eggs and a pinch of nutmeg to the mixture. Mix well and leave overnight.

Make the pasta dough by mixing together the eggs, flour and water. Knead together until the dough is smooth, then roll out the pasta sheets as thin as possible. Place small balls (about the size of a hazelnut) of the meat filling on the pasta dough about an inch away from one another.

Fold the sheet of pasta in half to cover the filling, making sure that the edges stick together well. There should be no air in the anolini, otherwise they may open during cooking.

Then cut the pasta using a circular pasta cutter, so that in the center of each anolino there is the ball of filling. The anolini are cooked and served in meat broth.

Maltagliati con i fagioli
Maltagliati with bean soup

Servings 4
Difficulty Low
Region Emilia Romagna

Meat

For the pasta: 10½ oz (300 g) all-purpose flour – 3 eggs.
For the soup: 10½ oz (300 g) borlotti beans, dried – 3½ oz (100 g) onion – 1 clove of garlic – 3½ oz (100 g) lardo (bacon fat) – 1½ oz (40 g) tomato paste – 2⅔ tablespoons (4 cl) extra virgin olive oil – 1 piece of ham skin – 5⅓ pints (2.5 liters) water, lukewarm – 1½ oz (40 g) grated Parmigiano Reggiano cheese – salt and pepper.

15 minutes preparation time + 50 minutes cooking time + 12 h soaking time

Leave the beans to soak for 12 hours in cold water with a pinch of bicarbonate to soften the skin. Put the flour on a work surface and make a well, add the eggs and make a uniform dough. Leave to rest for 20 minutes.

Roll out the pasta into fairly thin sheets, flour and then fold over and over again and then cut fettuccine about ⅓ inch (1 cm) wide. Spread the fettuccine on a lightly floured tray and leave to dry. Then cut the pasta with a knife and break with your hands to obtain pieces of pasta about ⅔ inch (2 cm) long.

Chop the bacon and the onion finely. Put them in a large pot over a medium heat, add ⅓ of the oil, sauté the onion and the bacon. Add the tomato paste, the beans, the ham skin and 5⅓ pints (2.5 liters) lukewarm water. When the beans are cooked (about 45 minutes) remove about half of them, purée them and return them to the pan. Bring back to the boil, add the maltaglitati and cook. Serve hot with plenty of grated Parmesan cheese and the rest of the extra virgin olive oil.

Minestra con carciofi e pancetta
Artichoke and bacon soup

Servings 4
Difficulty Low

Meat

4¼ cups (1 liter) chicken broth – 6 artichokes – 3 tablespoons lemon juice – 4 tablespoons extra virgin olive oil – 1 clove of garlic, crushed – 5⅓ oz (150 g) bacon, cubed – 2⅛ oz (60 g) onion, chopped – 14⅛ oz (400 g) pastina (small pasta) (e.g. lancette) – 2¾ oz (80 g) grated Parmigiano Reggiano cheese.

15 minutes preparation time + 35 minutes cooking time

Heat chicken broth in a medium sized pot over low heat until it is very hot. Leave to simmer on lowest heat until needed.

Clean artichokes by slicing at least ¼ inch (0.5 cm) off the top and bottom and remove all the tough outer leaves. Cut artichoke in half lengthwise and remove the choke.

Cut into thin slices and soak in a bowl of water with lemon juice to prevent the artichokes turning black. Heat 2 tablespoons olive oil in a large skillet over medium high heat. Add garlic and drained artichoke slices and sauté for 5-6 minutes. Remove from pan and set aside.

In same skillet, add bacon and sauté over medium high heat until lightly browned. Remove from pan and set aside. Add remaining 2 tablespoons olive oil to skillet.

Add onions and sauté for 2-3 minutes. Add the pastina and enough hot chicken broth to cover pasta. Cook continuously, adding more broth as needed until pasta is cooked.

Add artichokes a few minutes before the end of cooking. When pasta is cooked and the excess broth has evaporated, stir in cheese, bacon and butter.

Transfer to a serving dish and serve hot.

Minestra di patate allo zafferano
Potato soup with saffron

Servings 6
Difficulty Low
Region Abruzzo

Vegetable

1 ⅓ lb (600 g) potatoes – 10½ oz (300 g) cannarozzetti or spaghetti broken into small pieces – ½ onion – 1 carrot – celery – saffron from L'Aquila in threads – 4¼ tablespoons (7 cl) extra virgin olive oil – salt.

30 minutes preparation time + 10 minutes cooking time

Lightly sauté the onion, carrot and celery in olive oil. As soon as the mixture has cooled, add the saffron threads, mixing well, and then leave to rest. Boil and peel the potatoes and dice them.
Pour 8 cups (2 l) of water into the pot containing the saffron mixture, add the potatoes and then add the salt. Bring to the boil and add the pasta. When the pasta is cooked, the soup will be ready to serve, preferably after leaving it to rest for a while.
This soup is also delicious without the pasta, but in this case use less water.

Did you know that…
Saffron is a spice derived from the flower of the Crocus Sativus. It is grown all over Italy but above all in Abruzzo and Sardinia. Saffron has an unmistakable yellow color and is widely used in Italian cuisine (for example in risotto alla milanese – Milanese style risotto). Saffron is considered a very precious spice and the flowers from which it is made are still picked and separated by hand. It takes up to 120000 flowers to produce a kilo of pure saffron.

Passatelli
Passatelli

Servings 4
Difficulty Low
Region Emilia Romagna

Vegetable

8¾ oz (250 g) grated Parmigiano Reggiano cheese – 7 oz (200 g) breadcrumbs – ¾ oz (20 g) butter – 1¼ oz (35 g) flour – 4 eggs – 8½ cups (2 l) broth – nutmeg – salt.

30 minutes preparation time + 5 minutes cooking time

Mix the eggs, the breadcrumbs, 5⅓ oz (150 g) of the Parmigiano Reggiano cheese, the butter, the flour, salt, pepper and the nutmeg to make the passatelli. Wrap up the dough in plastic wrap or cling film and leave to rest for about 20 minutes.

Bring the broth (preferably capon broth) to the boil in a pan. With the aid of a potato ricer, or, if available the special utensil with a disk that has larger holes, pass all of the mixture through to obtain strips the length of a finger letting them drop directly into the broth. Cook and serve in bowls together with the broth and a generous helping of grated Parmigiano Reggiano cheese.

Did you know that...
Nutmeg is one of the most cherished spices in traditional Italian cuisine.
Nutmeg is the seed of the fruit of the Myrustica Fragrans, an evergreen tree originally from an atoll in the Pacific Ocean and cultivated in different places along the equator. Indeed, for some time, the nutmeg tree grew exclusively on the slopes of the volcanic island of Run, one of the Banda Islands, in the Molucca Archipelago.

Pasta e ceci alla romana
Pasta with chickpeas

Servings 4
Difficulty Medium
Region Latium

Vegetable

5⅓ oz (150 g) pasta (cannolicchi) – 10½ oz (300 g) chickpeas – 1 clove of garlic – 2 salted anchovies – extra virgin olive oil – rosemary – 1 oz (30 g) concentrated tomato sauce – salt – pepper.

30 minutes preparation time + 1 hour and 30 minutes cooking time

Leave the chickpeas to soak the day before cooking. Boil the chickpeas in salted water with the rosemary. They should cook for about one and a half hours.
In another pan, put 4 tablespoons of oil, the chopped garlic and the cleaned chopped anchovies. Sauté and then add the tomato sauce that you have diluted in a little of the cooking water from the chickpeas. Cook for 10 minutes and pour in the chickpeas with their cooking water, having removed the rosemary. Bring to the boil, add the pasta and cook. The soup should be quite thick and should be served with freshly ground black pepper.

Did you know that…
Today chickpeas are among the most common pulses in the world, particularly so in the Middle East and in India.
In Italy chickpeas are mostly grown in the central regions. They derive from the wild chickpea plant, which probably originated in Turkey. The oldest records regarding the cultivation of chickpeas are from modern Iraq, from where they spread all over the Ancient World. They were certainly known in Ancient Egypt where they were given to the slaves to eat, as well as in Ancient Greece and Ancient Rome.

Quadrucci con piselli
Egg pasta with peas

Servings 4
Difficulty **Medium**
Region **Abruzzo**

Vegetable

10½ oz (300 g) flour – 3 eggs – 3½ tablespoons (5 cl) white wine – 1 onion – 1¾
lb (800 g) fresh peas – 7 oz (200 g) bacon – salt to taste.

30 minutes preparation time + 30 minutes cooking time

Mix the flour and the eggs to make a smooth dough. Cover and leave the dough to rest for about 20 minutes. Roll the pasta out into thin sheets, cut it into strips ⅓ inch (1 cm) wide and then cut into squares. Leave the squares to dry on a well floured tray.

Sauté the finely chopped onion in the oil over a medium heat, add the bacon and gently fry for a few minutes, add the white wine and cook until it evaporates completely.

Add the peas and cover with water. Simmer for about 20 minutes and then add the "quadrucci." Adjust the salt and continue cooking over a medium heat until the pasta is ready to be served. The "quadrucci" should be served in a little of the broth or cooking liquid.

Vellutata di carciofi
Artichoke velouté

Servings 4
Difficulty Low

Vegetable

8 artichokes – juice of 1 lemon – 8½ cups (2 l) vegetable broth – ¾ oz (20 g) rice starch – 1¾ oz (50 g) butter – 2 egg yolks – 1¾ oz (50 g) Parmesan cheese, grated – salt.

20 minutes preparation + 20 minutes cooking time

Cut off the top part of the artichokes, remove the tougher external leaves, cut them into 4 segments and remove the choke. Put them in water and lemon juice to avoid them turning black.
Heat the butter in a large frying pan over a medium heat and when it has melted, add the rice starch and cook for a few minutes. Add the strained artichokes and the vegetable broth. When the bottom part of the artichokes is cooked, blend everything in a food processor and season with salt. Pass the velouté through a sieve to remove any filaments from the leaves. Lastly add the egg yolks and the Parmesan cheese.
Mix well so that all the ingredients are thoroughly blended, using a wooden spoon and serve hot.
You can serve this dish with croutons and a little of extra virgin olive oil.

Zuppa di finocchi
Fennel soup

Servings 4
Difficulty *Low*
Region *Sardinia*

Vegetable

10$\frac{1}{2}$ oz (300 g) saffron bread – 14$\frac{1}{8}$ oz (400 g) fennel – 7 oz (200 g) fresh sliced Pecorino cheese – 1 oz (30 g) butter – 3$\frac{1}{2}$ tablespoons (5 cl) extra virgin olive oil – salt and pepper.

30 minutes preparation time + 20 minutes cooking time

Wash the fennel well under running water, cut it à la julienne. Heat a large pan full of water and when it boils, add salt and the fennel. Meanwhile, cut the bread into slices $\frac{1}{2}$ inch (1.5 cm) thick. Sauté the slices of bread in half the butter and oil in a frying pan.

As soon as the fennel is cooked, put half of it in an oven-dish, then put the bread on top and cover with half of the slices of cheese. Put the rest of the fennel on top, add a little salt, freshly ground pepper and finish with the rest of the cheese. Then pour over two ladles of the cooking water from the fennel and finish by dotting some small flakes of butter on top.

Bake in a hot oven at 400°F (200°C) and leave until the cheese has melted and formed a light golden crust.

Serve immediately.

Regional name: Suppa de frenucu

Zuppa di merluzzi e patate
Cod and potato soup

Servings 4
Difficulty Low
Region Molise

Fish

2⅓ lb (1 kg) potatoes – 4 cod – ⅝ cup (1.5 dl) extra virgin olive oil – 2 cloves of garlic – 3 tablespoons parsley, chopped – salt.

30 minutes preparation time + 25 minutes cooking time

Remove the insides of the cod and the gills and wash them thoroughly. Peel the potatoes, wash them and cut into disks. Sauté the potatoes with the garlic in the oil over a low heat and then add the potatoes, cover with water and simmer for about 15 minutes after water begins to boil. Add the cod and cook for a further 10 minutes. Season with salt. Before serving, sprinkle with chopped parsley.

Zuppa di pesce
Fish stew

Servings 4
Difficulty Low
Region Veneto

Fish

2²⁄₃ lb (1.2 kg) fish (prawns, rock fish, gurnard, sea bass, smooth hound, clams, etc.) – 2¹⁄₈ cups (50 cl) white wine – ½ lemon – 1 stalk celery – 1 onion, chopped – 1 carrot – 1 tomato – 1¾ oz (50 g) butter – 3½ tablespoons (5 cl) olive oil – 1 clove of garlic, chopped – 3 tablespoons parsley, chopped – 1¾ oz (50 g) tomato sauce – salt – pepper.

40 minutes preparation time + 50 minutes cooking time

Clean and wash the fish and boil it 6¹⁄₃ pints (3 liters) of water with the white wine, the lemon, the celery, the carrot, the tomato and the whole onion.

Once cooked, drain and fillet the fish. Heat the butter and oil in a large skillet over a medium heat. Sauté the onion and garlic for about 2 minutes. Add the fish and simmer for a further 2 minutes so that it gains flavor. Add the tomato sauce and cook for a further 10 minutes. Add salt and pepper to taste.

Strain the fish stock and add to the fish in the pan the quantity necessary to obtain the consistency of a thick soup and cook for a further 10 minutes.

Add a sprinkling of chopped parsley and serve.

Zuppa di zucca
Pumpkin soup

Servings 6
Difficulty **Medium**
Region **Lombardy**

Vegetable

4 lb (1.8 kg) pumpkin – 2⅛ oz (60 g) grated Parmigiano Reggiano cheese – 2 table-spoons parsley, chopped – 4 leaves of basil – 1 stalk of celery – 2 sprigs thyme – 1 clove of garlic – vegetable broth – 1 oz (30 g) butter – salt and pepper.

20 minutes preparation time + 2 hours cooking time

Cut off the top cap of the pumpkin, remove all the seeds and filaments, thus obtaining a sort of soup tureen complete with its lid. Gently fry the chopped parsley, a few basil leaves and two sprigs of thyme in butter for approximately 2-3 minutes. Pour the stock, the sautéed herbs, garlic, grated cheese, salt and pepper into the pumpkin, stir well and put the lid on, fitting it tightly so that the pumpkin is sealed.

Bake at 450°F (230°C) for two hours or so. Take the pumpkin to the table on a plate, take off the lid, remove the garlic, and, with a serving spoon, scrape away the pumpkin flesh and mix it slowly with the stock, to make a soup. If the soup is too thick, add some more hot stock. Serve hot.

MAIN COURSES

IN ALL MEALS, EVEN THOSE COOKED AT HOME, BUT EVEN MORE SO WHEN THERE ARE MEALS ON IMPORTANT OCCASIONS, THE COURSE THAT FOLLOWS THE FIRST COURSE, BE IT A FIRST COURSE OF SOUP OR PASTA, IS THE CENTRAL MOST IMPORTANT ELEMENT OF THE MEAL. ACCORDING TO PERSONAL TASTE AND LOCAL TRADITION, THIS MAY BE MEAT, FISH OR VARIOUS EGG DISHES, BUT IT CAN ALSO BE A PIZZA OR A PIE, FLAN OR SOUFFLÉ. EVEN COLD CUTS AND SAUSAGES (TYPICAL AT CERTAIN TIMES OF THE YEAR) AND CHEESE, CAN BE SERVED AS A MAIN COURSE.

MEAT DISHES ARE THE MOST IMPORTANT AND INCLUDE GAME (FEATHER AND FUR), FARM ANIMALS (HERE AGAIN BOTH FEATHER AND FUR), LAMB, GOAT, MUTTON AND GOAT, USED IN SOME REGIONS AND AT CERTAIN TIMES OF THE YEAR, BEEF, VEAL AND PORK. IN REGIONAL CUISINE THERE ARE MANY RECIPES EVEN FOR OFFAL THAT IS USUALLY PREPARED IN A VERY COMPLEX BUT TASTY WAY.

GAME IS THE REALM OF AFICIONADOS, HUNTERS OR, VERY OFTEN, RESTAURANTEURS WHO ADOPT IT IS A SPECIALTY OF THEIR RESTAURANT. GAME REQUIRES SPECIAL SKILL TO PREPARE AND COOK. THERE ARE VARIOUS RECIPES; PATÉ, ROAST, STEW OR SALMÌ THAT ARE OFTEN ACCOMPANIED BY CROUTONS OR SOFT OR GRILLED POLENTA.

THERE ARE MANY RECIPES FOR THE MEAT FROM FARM ANIMALS. THESE FALL UNDER WHITE MEATS SUCH AS CHICKEN, TURKEY AND RABBIT AND DARKER MEATS AND IN SOME CASES MEATS WITH HIGHER FAT CONTENT SUCH AS GOOSE, DUCK, GUINEA FOWL AND PIGEON. THESE ARE USUALLY PREPARED AS ROAST, IN SALMÌ, BOILED (RICH BOILED MEAT DISHES WITH DIFFERENT SAUCES), FRIED, SPIT-ROASTED, COOKED IN EARTHENWARE POTS, COOKED IN SALT OR GRILLED. VERY OFTEN, WITH POULTRY IN PARTICULAR, SPICY STUFFING IS USED, BUT THERE ARE ALSO RECIPES WITH INGREDIENTS SUCH AS WINE, HERBS, GARLIC BASED SAUCES, CREAM, MILK, EGGS, OLIVES, MUSTARD, AND ALL SORTS OF FRUIT SUCH AS PRUNES, GRAPES, APPLES AND ORANGES, AND ALSO MUSHROOMS AND TRUFFLES... THE NOBLER MEATS SUCH AS BEEF AND VEAL BUT ALSO THE TASTIER PORK, LEND THEMSELVES TO A WIDE VARIETY OF PREPARATIONS: BOILING, BRAISING AND COOK-ING THOROUGHLY BUT VERY SLOWLY, VARIOUS TYPES OF STEW BUT ALSO LIGHTER PREPARATIONS THAT ARE MORE SUITED FOR THE SUMMER SUCH AS *CARPACCIO* AND MEAT *TARTARE*, *VITELLO TONNATO* (COLD VEAL WITH TUNA SAUCE) AND *ROAST-BEEF*, BARBEQUED RIB STEAKS, AND ALSO SLICED STEAK, ESCALOPES, MEAT ROLLS, MEAT

BALLS AND MEAT LOAF. FISH IS JUST AS IMPORTANT AS MEAT FOR THE SECOND COURSE: SOMETIMES IT IS EVEN MORE APPRECIATED BECAUSE IT IS LIGHTER, MORE EASILY DIGESTED, AND CERTAINLY BECAUSE OF THE WIDE VARIETY OF FLAVORS AND NUMEROUS RECIPES. THE LARGE AND MEDIUM SIZED FISH, THAT ARE THE SOURCE OF INSPIRATION FOR MANY REFINED RECIPES, COME FROM THE SEA; FISH THAT IS TYPI-CALLY KNOWN AS *PESCE AZZURRO*, OR DARK BLUE COLORED FISH, THAT GIVE RISE TO TASTY AND FLAVORFUL RECIPES. CRUSTACEANS AND SHELLFISH, ALSO FROM THE SEA, ARE TYPICALLY DESTINED TO BECOME PART OF REFINED DISHES. IN SOME LAND LOCKED REGIONS WHERE THERE ARE LAKES AND RIVERS, VARIOUS SPECIES OF FRESH WATER FISH ARE USED. REGIONAL RECIPES ARE USUALLY KNOWN BY THEIR PACE NAME APPELLATION SUCH AS "ALLA LIVORNESE," "ALLA NAPOLETANA," "ALLA FIORENTINA," "ALLA SICILIANA," MEANING LEGHORNIAN, NEAPOLITAN, FLORENTINE OR SICILIAN "STYLE," THAT LINK THEM WITH THEIR PLACE OF ORIGIN. FISH IS PREPARED IN MANY DIFFERENT WAYS: *ALLA MUGNAIA* (THE MILLER'S WAY), SOUSED, MARINATED, FRIED, BOILED, GRILLED, OVEN BAKED, BAKED IN TINFOIL, STEWED, IN SWEET AND SOUR SAUCE: ALL METHODS THAT BRING OUT THE BEST IN IT.

MAIN COURSES

Meat

Agnello al sugo bianco *Lamb in white sauce*	230
Agnello cacio e uovo alla molisana *Lamb, cheese and eggs from Molise*	232
Agnello di Pasqua *Easter lamb*	234
Arista alla toscana ai profumi del sottobosco con fagioli all'olio di frantoio *Tuscan roast loin of pork with mushrooms, beans and fresh olive oil*	236
Arrosticini *Barbequed mutton*	238
Arrosto di vitello al latte *Roast veal in milk*	240
Bistecca del curato *Umbrian style veal chops*	242
Bocconcini di maiale al prosciutto profumati al balsamico *Pork fillet with ham and balsamic vinegar of Modena*	244
Brasato di manzo al Barolo *Braised beef in Barolo*	246
Coiettas *Sardinian meat rolls*	248
Coniglio all'ischitana *Rabbit Ischia-style*	250
Coniglio alla sanremasca *Rabbit San Remo-style*	252
Coniglio con peperoni e olive *Rabbit with peppers and olives*	254
Costata di manzo con cipolle *Beef rib steaks with onions*	256
Costine di maiale alla montanara *Pork spare ribs with polenta*	258
Cotoletta alla milanese *Milanese veal cutlet*	260

Agnello al sugo bianco
Lamb in white sauce

Servings 4
Difficulty **Medium**
Region **Sardinia**

Meat

2¼ lb (1 kg) lamb – 1 onion – ⅓ cup (8 cl) extra virgin olive oil – 4 eggs – lemon juice – salt – pepper.

1 hour preparation time + 20 minutes cooking time

Beat the eggs in a steel bowl and blend in the lemon juice. Heat a pan of water over a medium heat and, when the water boils, cook the egg mixture in a bain marie, stirring often with a whisk.
Cut the lamb into pieces and wash with cold water. Put the oil, lamb salt, pepper and the julienned onion in a pot over a medium heat. Lower the heat, the lamb must not brown, cover with a lid and leave to cook, stirring often.
When the meat is cooked, pour over the egg sauce and serve.

Agnello cacio e uovo alla molisana
Lamb, cheese and eggs from Molise

Servings 4
Difficulty Medium
Region Molise

Meat

2¼ lb (1 kg) baby lamb – 3½ oz (100 g) Parma ham – 1 cup (2.5 dl) dry white wine – ⅞ oz (25 g) lard – ½ cup (1 dl) broth – 1 onion – all–purpose flour – nutmeg – 3 eggs – ½ lemon – salt – pepper.

30 minutes preparation time + 1 hour cooking time

Put the lard, the ham and the onion cut into thin slices in a large pan. Gently fry, add salt, pepper and add a pinch of nutmeg.

Cut the lamb into chunks and after coating in flour, add to the pan and sauté. Pour in the stock. As soon as it has reduced, add the white wine, salt, pepper and cook over low heat.

When the lamb is well cooked, arrange on a hot serving plate.

Pour the juices from the meat into a small pan and blend in three beaten yolks together with the juice of half a lemon. Mix and leave over low heat for a minute, then pour the sauce over the meat. Bake at 350°F (180°C) until a golden crust forms. Serve immediately.

Agnello di Pasqua
Easter lamb

Servings 4
Difficulty **Medium**
Region **Apulia**

Meat

2¼ lb (1 kg) lamb – 14⅛ oz (400 g) fresh, very tender peas – 1 onion – 2 eggs – 1¾ oz (50 g) grated Pecorino cheese – ½ cup (1 dl) dry white wine – ⅓ cup (8 cl) extra virgin olive oil – 1 tablespoon parsley, chopped – salt and pepper.

20 minutes preparation time + 1 hour cooking time

Cut the lamb up into medium sized pieces.

Fry the chopped onion in the oil in a pot over a medium flame and brown lightly. Add the lamb and gently fry it, turning very frequently. Add the white wine, cover the pot and cook in the oven at 350°F (180°C) for approximately 40 minutes. When it is ¾ cooked, add the peas and continue to cook. Beat the eggs in a bowl and mix in the Pecorino cheese and the parsley.

When the lamb is cooked, pour the egg mixture on top and wait until it thickens before serving.

Arista alla toscana ai profumi del sottobosco con fagioli all'olio di frantoio
Tuscan roast loin of pork with mushrooms, beans and fresh olive oil

Servings 4
Difficulty Medium
Region Tuscany

Meat

1¾ lb (800 g) loin of pork – 1¾ oz (50 g) dried mushrooms – 2¾ oz (80 g) carrot – 2¾ oz (80 g) celery – 1 teaspoon parsley, chopped – 5⅓ oz (150 g) dried beans – 1 teaspoon fennel seeds – 1 teaspoon sage, chopped – 2 cloves of garlic – black pepper to taste – 1 cup (2.5 dl) white wine – 4¼ cups (1 l) vegetable stock – 1 cup (2.5 dl) brown stock – 1 sprig rosemary, salt.

30 minutes preparation time + 1 hour cooking time

Put the beans to soak in water the evening before.

Tie the pork loin with food string. Tie it tightly so that it does not loosen during cooking.

Chop the rosemary, garlic, sage and fennel seeds, add salt and freshly ground black pepper to the mixture. Make small holes in the meat with a fine-blade knife, insert the mixture in these holes.

This seasoning will also add flavor to the inside of the meat.

Pour oil into a large casserole and braise the pork over a medium heat, taking care to turn it occasionally. While it is cooking, add some white wine and reduce. Remember to add boiling broth to the pork as it is cooking. Cook for about 1 hour.

In a large casserole, soften the chopped garlic by frying gently in oil, then add the beans. Season with salt and pepper, cover with water and cook.

In another pan, sauté the chopped vegetables in a drop of oil. Add the dried mushrooms (which have been soaked in cold water), the chopped parsley and some white wine and cook until it reduces. Add the brown stock, season with salt and pepper, cook for 5 minutes.

When the pork is cooked, slice and arrange on a plate and pour both sauces over the slices, the one with the beans and the one with the mushrooms.

Arrosticini
Barbequed mutton

Servings 4
Difficulty **Low**
Region **Abruzzo**

Meat

2¼ lb (1 kg) mutton (wether) – pepper – salt (only at the end.
15 minutes preparation time + 10 minutes cooking time

Cut the meat up into little pieces to put onto 8 – 12 inch (20-30 cm) wooden skewers. The skewers are then roasted over charcoal at a low heat.
The traditional recipe calls exclusively for wether mutton and alternative cooking methods should be avoided (such as using a hotplate or cooking in the oven). Meat cooked in this way can be accompanied with traditional home made bread dipped in olive oil.

Arrosto di vitello al latte
Roast veal in milk

Servings 4
Difficulty **Low**
Region **Lombardy**

Meat

1 ¾ lb (800 g) veal rump – 1 ¾ oz (50 g) Parma ham – 1 ¾ oz (50 g) butter – 4 ¼ cups (1 l) milk – 1 ¾ oz (50 g) all-purpose flour – salt to taste.

20 minutes preparation time + 40 minutes cooking time

Sauté the finely chopped ham in the butter over a medium heat. Add the veal seasoned with salt and pepper and fry gently. Add the flour and cook for a couple of minutes. Add some of the milk and leave to cook, adding more milk during cooking so that the meat is not left dry. When the veal is cooked, slice and serve in the sauce obtained from the cooking juices.
Instead of veal you can use beef.

Bistecca del curato
Umbrian style veal chops

Servings 4
Difficulty **Medium**
Region **Umbria**

Meat

4 veal chops – 1 small bunch basil – 1 tablespoon fresh chopped marjoram – 5 cloves of garlic – ½ small onion, small – 4 leaves of mint – 1 sprig rosemary – 1 pinch mustard powder – 2 salted anchovies – 5 lemons – 2 tablespoons (3 cl) white wine vinegar – 2½ tablespoons (4 cl) extra virgin olive oil – salt and pepper.

15 minutes preparation time + 15 minutes cooking time

Cook the veal chops, which have been seasoned with salt and pepper, on both sides in a pan with a drop of oil.

In a mortar, pound all the herbs together with the vinegar, lemon juice and the boned, desalted anchovies which have been cut into pieces.

When the veal chops are cooked, remove from the heat pour the sauce into the pan and serve immediately.

Bistecca del curato
Umbrian style veal chops

Servings 4
Difficulty Medium
Region Umbria

Meat

4 veal chops – 1 small bunch basil – 1 tablespoon fresh chopped marjoram – 5 cloves of garlic – ½ small onion, small – 4 leaves of mint – 1 sprig rosemary – 1 pinch mustard powder – 2 salted anchovies – 5 lemons – 2 tablespoons (3 cl) white wine vinegar – 2½ tablespoons (4 cl) extra virgin olive oil – salt and pepper.

15 minutes preparation time + 15 minutes cooking time

Cook the veal chops, which have been seasoned with salt and pepper, on both sides in a pan with a drop of oil.
In a mortar, pound all the herbs together with the vinegar, lemon juice and the boned, desalted anchovies which have been cut into pieces.
When the veal chops are cooked, remove from the heat pour the sauce into the pan and serve immediately.

Bocconcini di maiale al prosciutto profumati al balsamico
Pork fillet with ham and balsamic vinegar of Modena

Servings 4
Difficulty *Low*
Region *Emilia Romagna*

Meat

2 pork fillets, (of about 1⅔ lb (750 g) – 12 slices Parma ham – Balsamic Vinager of Modena – 1 sprig rosemary – 2 cloves of garlic – ⅝ lb (300 g) baby salad – extra virgin olive oil – salt – pepper.

20 minutes preparation time + 20 minutes cooking time

Begin by removing the excess fat from the slices of ham. Cut the pork fillet into small pieces, about 2 oz (60 g) each. Wrap each piece of pork in a slice of ham, fixing it in place with a toothpick. Heat a little olive oil in a frying pan, add the rosemary and the garlic and the pieces of pork.
Drizzle the meat with the balsamic vinegar according to your taste. Cook the meat on both sides until the center is no longer pink. Before serving, place the meat on a bed of lettuce, season with salt, freshly ground black pepper and olive oil. Pour over the reduced balsamic vinegar sauce.

Did you know that...
In the 1st century AD, Marco Terenzio Varrone wrote: "It is believed that Nature gave the pig to Man in order for him to live well." This quote demonstrates the high opinion Europeans have always held of the pig.

Brasato di manzo al Barolo
Braised beef in Barolo

Servings 4
Difficulty **Medium**
Region **Piedmont**

Meat

3 ½ lb (1.5 kg) beef brisket – 1 bottle Barolo wine – 1 onion – 1 carrot – 1 stalk celery – 2 bay leaves – 1 sprig rosemary – 5 black pepper corns – 1 ½ oz (40 g) butter – 1 ½ oz (40 g) Parma ham fat – potato starch as required – 2 cloves of garlic – salt to taste.

30 minutes preparation time + 2 hours and 30 minutes cooking time + 24 hours marinating time

Place the beef in a deep bowl and pour a bottle of Barolo over it. Add the sliced onion and carrot, a little chopped celery, two bay leaves, a pinch of black pepper corns. Leave the beef to marinate for 24 hours, turning it every few hours.

When you are ready to cook the meat, remove it from the marinade and dry it. Tie it up with kitchen string to keep the shape and place it in a saucepan with a little butter, the ham fat, garlic and rosemary. Brown the meat on all sides.

In the meantime, sieve the marinade to remove the vegetables and herbs. Pour the sieved marinade into a saucepan and boil until it is reduced by one half. Season the meat, which should be nicely browned, with salt, add various ladles of the marinade. Cover and cook over a moderate heat.

Skim off the fat, using a small ladle and thicken the sauce with a little potato starch dissolved in a drop of water. Once the meat is cooked, gently remove the string and arrange it on a serving dish. Carefully slice the meat and pour the fond on top. Serve with mashed potatoes.

Coiettas
Sardinian meat rolls

Servings 4
Difficulty **Medium**
Region **Sardinia**

Meat

8 slices beef – 1¾ oz (50 g) lardo or bacon – 2 cloves of garlic – 1 sprig parsley – 1⅓ tablespoons (20 g) extra virgin olive oil – 1⅓ tablespoons (20 ml) white wine – ½ cup (100 ml) broth – salt and pepper.

20 minutes preparation time + 10 minutes cooking time

Using a meat hammer, beat the slices of meat until thin. Then season with salt and pepper.
Finely chop the garlic, parsley and lardo. Mix together and spread a little on each slice of meat. Roll up each slice of meat, forming a cylinder, and use a toothpick or kitchen string to secure it.
Sauté the meat rolls in a little oil, browning them on all sides. Once nicely browned, add the broth and continue cooking, covered, over very low heat. A few minutes before they are cooked, pour in 3 tablespoons of white wine. Cook uncovered for another few minutes, remove the toothpicks or string and serve.

Coniglio all'ischitana
Rabbit Ischia-style

Servings 4
Difficulty Medium
Region Campania

Meat

2¼ lb (1 kg) rabbit – 3½ tablespoons (5 cl) vinegar – 1 lb 1⅝ oz (500 g) cherry tomatoes – ½ cup (1 dl) white wine – ¼ cup (5 cl) extra virgin olive oil – 2 cloves of garlic – herbs (thyme, basil, rosemary, marjoram), chopped – chili pepper – salt.

20 minutes preparation time + 40 minutes cooking time

Cut the rabbit into small pieces: rinse in water and vinegar and dry. In a large pan, gently fry the un-peeled garlic in a drop of oil until golden. Remove and garlic and sauté the pieces of rabbit over a high flame so that they are browned all over.
Add the wine and cook until it evaporates. Add the cherry tomatoes cut into quarters, season with salt and pepper, and lastly add the herbs. Leave to cook for about half an hour. Serve hot.

Coniglio alla sanremasca
Rabbit San Remo-style

Servings 4
Difficulty **Medium**
Region **Liguria**

Meat

2¼ lb (1 kg) rabbit – 1 onion – 1 clove of garlic – 3 sprigs rosemary – 1½ oz (40 g) pine nuts – 3½ oz (100 g) San Remo olives (or small black olives) – 3½ tablespoons (5 cl) extra virgin olive oil – ⅞ cup (200 dl) dry white wine – broth – salt.

20 minutes preparation time + 40 minutes cooking time

Cut the rabbit into pieces, season with salt to taste and sauté in the oil in a saucepan. Add the chopped onion and soften. Splash with the wine and cook, adding a little stock if necessary.
Meanwhile grind the pine nuts, garlic, rosemary and pitted olives, saving fifteen whole ones. After cooking for about 30 minutes, add the chopped mixture and cook for another ten minutes, add whole olives and remove from the heat.
Serve warm.

Coniglio con peperoni e olive
Rabbit with peppers and olives

Servings 4
Difficulty *Medium*
Region **Apulia**

Meat

2¼ lb (1 kg) rabbit – 2 green peppers – 7 oz (200 g) extra virgin olive oil – 3½ oz (100 g) black olives – 1 onion – 1 cup (2 dl) dry white wine – salt and pepper.

20 minutes preparation time + 40 minutes cooking time

Cut the rabbit into pieces, sauté the chopped onion in oil in a large pan, add the rabbit and fry gently. Pour in the wine, allow it to evaporate, cover with a lid and continue to cook, adding a little water if necessary.

Meanwhile cut the peppers into diamond shaped pieces and sauté in a little oil over a medium heat. Add the peppers to the rabbit and then add the pitted olives. After about half an hour the rabbit should be cooked. Season with salt and pepper and serve hot.

Costata di manzo con cipolle
Beef rib steaks with onions

Servings 4
Difficulty Low
Region Trentino Alto Adige

Meat

4 well aged rib steaks – 2 large onions – 1 oz (30 g) butter – 1 oz (30 g) olive oil – ½ cup (1 dl) white wine – ¾ oz (20 g) all-purpose flour – salt and pepper.

15 minutes preparation time + 20 minutes cooking time

Lightly coat the steaks in flour. Finely slice the onions and brown slightly in a large pan containing butter and oil over a low heat. When the onions are golden add the steaks, raise the heat, splash with a little white wine, and season with salt and pepper.
When they have browned on one side, turn them over and finish cooking until the other side is also browned. Put the steaks on a serving plate and serve topped with the onions.

Did you know that...
Steak is such an ancient food that it is even pictured on the walls of the Etruscan tombs of Tarquinia. In Italy, "costata," or a rib steak, is one of the most common cuts for "bistecche" (steaks). In fact, the two terms have almost become synonymous.

Chef's tips
This most classic of steaks is an ideal accompaniment for with a full-bodied red wine, such as a good Chianti or Teroldengo.

Costine di maiale alla montanara
Pork spare ribs with polenta

Servings 4
Difficulty **Medium**
Region **Friuli Venezia Giulia**

Meat

2¼ lb (1 kg) slightly smoked pork spare ribs, cut into 2 – 2½ inch (5 – 6 cm) chunks – 1¾ oz (50 g) butter – 2½ cups (5 dl) white wine – 3½ oz (100 g) cornmeal – salt and pepper to taste – 2⅛ cups (5 dl) water.

20 minutes preparation time + 1 hour cooking time

Fry the spare ribs in an earthenware pot, in butter, salt and pepper for 30 minutes. Add the white wine and continue cooking over a low heat for 30 minutes, adding the 2⅛ cups (5 dl) of water into which the cornmeal has been dissolved.
Serve the ribs while still hot with polenta.

Cotoletta alla milanese
Milanese veal cutlet

Servings 4
Difficulty Low
Region Lombardy

Meat

4 veal cutlets cut as thick as the bone – 3   oz (100 g) butter – 2 eggs – 3   oz (100 g) flour – 7 oz (200 g) breadcrumbs – 1 lemon – salt.

15 minutes preparation time + 15 minutes cooking time

Make a few cuts in the outer skin of the cutlets, so that they do not curl up during cooking, and flatten with a meat pounder. Cover them with flour and pat them in order to remove the excess flour. Crack the eggs into a bowl and beat them without adding salt, then dip the cutlets in, one at the time holding them by the bone.

Coat them with coarse breadcrumbs (prepared earlier by roughly grating some stale bread): press the chops with the palm of your hand so that the bread coating sticks and does not come off during cooking. Melt the butter in a large saucepan, turn up the heat, and when the butter is golden brown fry the cutlets. Fry them for 7 or 8 minutes on each side (they must be tender and lightly golden), dry on kitchen paper, arrange on a serving plate, season with salt and garnish with lemon segments. These cutlets are also excellent eaten cold. For this dish you must use top quality veal: tradition requires that each chop must include the bone to which the meat is attached like a flag to its mast.

Did you know that...
The cotoletta, has ancient origins. As a matter of fact, it was listed as "lompolos cum panito" in the menu from the lunch offered by an abbot to the monks of Saint Ambrose in 1134.

Chef's tips
If you want to savor the Cotoletta alla Milanese you can cover the bone, with aluminum foil, allowing your guests to pick it up with their hands and eat with ease.

Faraona arrosto
Roast guinea fowl

Servings 4
Difficulty Medium
Region Emilia Romagna

Meat

2¼ lb (1 kg) guinea fowl – 1½ oz (40 g) butter – ¾ oz (20 g) Parma ham – 1 sprig sage – 1 sprig rosemary – salt – pepper.
10 minutes preparation time + 1 hour and 10 minutes cooking time

Clean the guinea fowl after carefully burning off the feather stubs. Stuff with the rosemary, sage, salt and pepper, the minced Parma ham and a quarter of the butter.
Tie the guinea fowl with kitchen string. Melt the remaining butter in a casserole, lay the guinea fowl in it, add salt, cover with a lid and cook it over a low heat for about 2 hours, turning it from time to time.
When it is cooked, remove the string, reduce the cooking liquid, sieve it and pour over the guinea fowl which you have cut into pieces. Serve hot.

Fegato alla veneziana con quenelles di polenta
Venetian-style liver with polenta dumplings

Servings 4
Difficulty Low
Region Veneto

Meat

1⅓ lb (600 g) calf's liver – ⅓ cup (8 cl) extra virgin olive oil – 3½ oz (100 g) butter – 1 lb 1⅝ oz (500 g) onion – meat broth – white wine – ½ cup (1.2 dl) meat stock – 1¾ oz (50 g) all-purpose flour – parsley – ⅓ oz (10 g) salt – 1 pinch black pepper
For the polenta: 4¼ cups (1 l) water – 8¾ oz (250 g) cornmeal.

30 minutes preparation time + 25 minutes cooking time

Chop up the onion à la julienne. Soften the onion over a medium heat in the oil and butter, add salt and pepper.

Cut the liver into thin strips and flour it. Add it to the onion and stir vigorously. Add the wine and let it evaporate. Add the meat stock, the parsley and the salt at at the end.

Meanwhile, boil the water, add salt, and sprinkle the cornmeal into the water while stirring with a whisk. Cook for 40 to 45 minutes stirring with a wooden spoon every so often.

When it is cooked, wet two spoons with water and and use them to form a number of quenelles or dumplings to serve with the liver.

The liver should cook over a high flame for a short time, otherwise it becomes hard. It is not absolutely necessary to use flour, but it does help to keep the liver soft and binds the sauce.

Chef's tips
Salt should be added at the end because it dehydrates the liver and makes it hard and stringy.

Filetto di manzo all'aceto balsamico
Beef fillet with balsamic vinegar

Servings 4
Difficulty Low
Region Emilia Romagna

Meat

1 ¾ lb (800 g) fillet of beef – 1 ½ oz (40 g) oz all-purpose flour – ¼ cup (6 cl) balsamic vinegar – 2 tablespoons (3 cl) tablespoon olive oil – ½ cup (1 dl) meat broth – salt – pepper.

20 minutes preparation time + 10 minutes cooking time

Cut the fillet into four 1 – 1 ½ inch (3 – 4 cm) thick slices, depending on the width of the meat. Coat in flour, and shake off any excess.

Heat the oil in a frying pan over a medium-high to high flame, and when it is hot cook the fillets which have already been seasoned with salt and pepper. Cook on both sides, then remove the fat and add the balsamic vinegar. When the vinegar has evaporated, remove the fillets from the pan, add the meat broth and reduce until it thickens. As soon as the sauce is cooked, pour on the fillets and serve.

Did you know that...
In the past, beef consumption was reserved for the upper classes. According to this tale, King James I attended a banquet in his honor. At the end of the dinner, after having eaten and drunk in abundance, the King paid homage to the best roast beef that he had ever eaten. He called for his sword and he knighted the roast "Sir Loin."

Grigliata di carne
Mixed grill

Servings 4
*Difficulty **Medium***

Meat

1 lb 1⅝ oz lb s (500 g) pork spare ribs – 7 oz (200 g) pork sausage – 5⅓ oz (150 g) turkey breast – 1 chicken – 5 oz (140 g) bacon – 1 red pepper – 1 onion – 10½ oz (300 g) lamb chops – 3 cups (7 dl) extra virgin olive oil – 2⅛ cups (5 dl) Traditional Balsamic Vinegar of Modena – juice of 1 lemon – 2 cloves of garlic – 1 sprig rosemary.

8 minutes preparation time + 30 minutes cooking time + 8 hours marinating time

Cut the turkey breast, sausage, bacon, red pepper and the onion into 1 inch (3 cm) chunks, put them in a bowl with about 1¼ cups (3 dl) of non-filtered extra virgin olive oil, rosemary and garlic. Leave to marinate for 8 hours and then thread the meat and vegetables onto wooden or metal skewers, alternating the meat and vegetables.

Cut the chicken open, down the back and leave to marinate in about 1¾ cups (4 dl) extra virgin olive oil, lemon juice, rosemary and garlic for 8 hours. Also marinate for 8 hours the lamb cutlets, in garlic rosemary and balsamic vinegar from Modena and the pork spare ribs with only garlic and rosemary. Heat the grill and, when it is ready, cook the meat.

Remember to season with salt only when the meat is cooked.

Gulasch della Val Pusteria
Val Pusteria-style goulash

Servings 4
*Difficulty **Medium***
*Region **Trentino Alto Adige***

Meat

1 ¾ lb (800 g) chuck beef – 5 onions – ⅞ cup (2 dl) red wine – 1 teaspoon paprika, red – ⅞ oz (25 g) all-purpose flour – 1 lemon zest – 1 sprig of rosemary – 1 bay leaf – 1 sprig of marjoram – 2 tablespoons (3 cl) olive oil – 1 oz (30 g) tomato paste – 1 clove of garlic – salt – pepper.

25 minutes preparation time + 2 hours and 15 minutes cooking time

Chop the onions and cut the meat cut into cubes, put them in a pan and sauté for a few minutes. Dissolve the flour and the paprika in a little water in a glass and pour over the meat. Pour over some red wine and simmer until it evaporates, then add the herbs, the grated lemon and the tomato paste and mix well. Add a glass of water, cover and leave to cook for at least 2 hours. If it becomes too dry, add a little water.

This dish can be served with polenta, boiled potatoes or flour dumplings.

Involtini sardi
Sardinian cabbage rolls

Servings 4
Difficulty Low
Region Sardegna

Meat

1⅓ lb (600 g) lean beef or pork – 1 savoy cabbage with large leaves – 2 tablespoons (3 cl) extra virgin olive oil – ⅞ cup (2 dl) white wine – 1 clove of garlic – 5 sage leaves – 3 tablespoons parsley, chopped – salt – pepper.

20 minutes preparation time + 20 minutes cooking time

Chop the garlic, sage, and parsley and mix with the chopped meat and then use the mixture to make small balls or cylinders about 1¼ inches (3 cm) long and ¾ inch (2 cm) wide.
Break off the cabbage leaves and wash. Blanch the savoy cabbage leaves in salted water, and then wrap around the prepared meat balls or cylinders.
Sauté the rolls lightly in a pan in the oil, add the dry white wine and simmer until it evaporates. Then cover and leave to cook, adding water if necessary.

Ossobuchi alla milanese
Ossobuco Milanese-style

Servings 4
Difficulty Medium
Region Lombardy

Meat

4 slices of ossobuco (veal shank on the bone) 10 – 14 oz (300-400 g) each – 3½ oz (100 g) onion – 3½ oz (100 g) butter – 1¾ oz (100 g) all-purpose flour – ½ cup (1 dl) dry white wine – 1 cup (2.5 dl) meat broth – 1 clove of garlic – 1 bunch of parsley – 1 sprig of rosemary – zest of half a lemon.

20 minutes preparation time+ 1 hour and 40 minutes cooking time

Flour the ossobuco. In a large saucepan, melt the butter and lightly fry the ossobuco seasoned with salt and pepper. Remove when they are cooked on both sides and put to one aside. In the same pan in which you cooked the meat, soften the onion cut à la julienne over a low heat.

Put the ossobuchi back in the pan, splash with white wine and cook until it evaporates.

Cover the ossobuco with broth, put the lid on the pan and leave to cook.

Prepare the gremolata: chop the garlic and parsley finely with the lemon rind and rosemary. This mixture will be used to sprinkle over the ossobuco once they are cooked.

Chef's tips
The ossobuco should be cut at their ends so that the nerves do not shrink during cooking and make the ossobuco lose its shape.

Parmigiana di melanzane
Eggplant parmigiana

Servings 4
Difficulty Medium
Region Apulia

Meat

1 lb 1⅝ oz (500 g) eggplant – 2¾ oz (80 g) all-purpose flour – 2 eggs – 10½ oz (300 g) tomato sauce – 3½ oz (100 g) mozzarella cheese – 3½ oz (100 g) grated Parmesan cheese – 3½ oz (100 g) pork sausages, fresh – 2 tablespoons (3 cl) extra virgin olive oil – cooking oil – salt.
30 minutes preparation time + 1 hour cooking time

Clean the eggplants then cut them into very thin slices. Dip the slices in flour and beaten egg, then fry in hot oil. Drain and dry on straw paper or kitchen paper.

Pour a thin layer of tomato sauce over the bottom of an oven-dish, then arrange a layer of eggplant slices. Cover with crumbled mozzarella and crumbled sausage, pour over some sauce, sprinkle with Parmesan cheese and add another layer of eggplants, continue in this way until you finish the ingredients; the last layer must be of eggplant slices.

Top with sauce and Parmesan cheese, then bake in the oven at 350°F (180°C) until the top has formed a golden crust. You can substitute the eggplants with zucchini. The preparation is the same, but the zucchini must be sliced lengthwise. You can also substitute the sausage with slices of Mortadella, by putting slices of Mortadella in a single layer.

Pollo alla cacciatora
Hunter style chicken

Servings 4
Difficulty *Low*
Region **Emilia Romagna**

Meat

1 free-range chicken – 1⅓ tablespoons (2 cl) extra virgin olive oil – 1 medium sized onion – ¾ oz (20 g) butter – ½ cup (1 dl) white wine – 8¾ oz (250 g) canned peeled tomatoes – 1 green (or yellow) pepper (emptied inside), chopped – salt and pepper.

30 minutes preparation time + 45 minutes cooking time

Peel and chop the onion and soften in the butter and oil in a frying pan over medium heat. Cut the chicken into 8 pieces and sauté in the frying pan. Pour in the white wine and let it evaporate. Add the tomatoes and the peppers cut a julienne. Add salt and pepper and cover with a lid. Cook over a low flame.

Pollo alla Marengo
Chicken Marengo

Servings 4
Difficulty *Low*
Region *Piedmont*

Meat

2½ lb (1.2 kg) chicken – 7 oz (200 g) mushrooms (or 25 dried mushrooms) – 3½ oz (100 g) extra virgin olive oil – 1 cup dry white wine – ½ cup Madeira wine (or dry Marsala) – 1 tablespoon flour – 1 lemon – 1 small bunch parsley, chopped – salt and pepper.

30 minutes preparation time + 45 minutes cooking time

Divide the chicken into pieces (if you are using legs only, separate the thighs from the drumsticks). Clean the fresh mushrooms thoroughly or soak the dried ones in water.
Add about 1¾ tablespoons (25 g) of oil to the water and cook the mushrooms. Season to taste.
In a pan, cook the chicken pieces in the remaining oil. Once they are browned, season with salt and pepper and add the white wine. Complete the cooking. Spoon nearly all the cooking juice into a small saucepan. If it is too thick, dilute it with a little water.
Add the flour and Madeira wine, to obtain a smooth thick sauce. Add the mushrooms to the chicken, cook for a few minutes, pour in the sauce, then transfer everything into a hot dish and serve immediately. Sprinkle with chopped parsley and drizzle with lemon juice.

Rosa di Parma
Rosa di Parma fillet

Servings 4
Difficulty **Medium**
Region **Emilia Romagna**

Meat

1 ⅓ lb (600 g) beef fillet – 1 ¾ oz (50 g) Parmesan cheese, in slivers – 6 slices Parma ham – 3 cloves of garlic – 1 sprig rosemary – 3 ⅓ cups (75 cl) Lambrusco – 1 cup (25 cl) Marsala wine – 3 ½ oz (100 g) cream – ½ cup (1 dl) olive oil – ⅞ oz (25 g) butter – salt and pepper.

25 minutes preparation time + 20 minutes cooking time'

Open the fillet out with a knife like a book and then pound with a meat pounder, to form a large slice. Season with salt and pepper. Cover the slice of fillet with the slices of Parma ham and slivers of Parmesan, roll up and tie like a roast with kitchen string or netting. Sauté the fillet on all sides in a pan over a high flame in butter and oil with the chopped garlic and rosemary (the garlic can be left whole and removed after being sautéed). Add the red wine (Lambrusco) and the Marsala and leave to cook for about 20 minutes. Remove the fillet from the casserole. Pour the cream into the cooking liquid, raise the heat and cook for a few minutes to reduce the sauce. Season with salt and pepper to taste. Untie the fillet, cut into slices and cover with the sauce before serving.

Did you know that...
Lambrusco is a ruby-red light Italian sparkling wine with a low alcohol content. Lambrusco is one of the symbols of the Emilia region, and probably originates from a variety of wild grape. Indeed, the word "lambrusco" comes from the Latin words labrum meaning edge, and ruscum, a wild plant. The wine also has ancient origins, dating back more than two thousand years, proven by the fact that both Virgil and Cato both wrote about the wine. It seems as though Lambrusco was very popular in ancient Rome.

Saltimbocca alla romana
Saltimbocca Roman-style

Servings 4
Difficulty Low
Region Latium

Meat

8 escalopes of veal – 8 slices of Parma ham – 1¾ oz (50 g) butter – ½ cup (1 dl) white wine, dry – ⅓ oz (10 g) sage – 2⅛ oz (60 g) flour – salt and pepper.
10 minutes preparation time + 10 minutes cooking time

Cut the slices of veal and season with salt and pepper. On top of each slice of veal, place a slice of ham and a sage leaf, after washing and drying it, and fix with a cocktail stick.

Flour the saltimbocca on the side of the meat. Melt the butter in a large saucepan, add the saltimbocca and sauté for a few minutes only on the floured side. Splash with the white wine, cook for a few minutes until it evaporates. Arrange the saltimbocca on a serving dish and pour over the meat juices.

Chef's tips
Before preparing the slices of meat with ham and rosemary, they should be lightly beaten. The slices of meat should be floured at the last minute, just before being sautéed in the pan.

Spezzatino di vitello con patate
Veal stew with potatoes

Servings 4
Difficulty Low
Region Friuli Venezia Giulia

Meat

1 ¾ lb (800 g) lean veal – 1 carrot – 1 onion – 2 ¾ oz (80 g) tomato sauce – ½ cup (1 dl) white wine – 4 potatoes – 1 ¾ oz (50 g) butter – 2 tablespoons (3 cl) extra virgin olive oil – salt – pepper – 2 ⅛ oz (60 g) flour.

20 minutes preparation time + 45 minutes cooking time

Sauté the very thinly sliced carrot and onion in butter and oil, add the diced lightly floured meat and fry gently. Add a glass of white wine, the tomato sauce, salt and pepper. When the liquid has reduced, add the potatoes in pieces. Cover with water and cook uncovered for 45-50 minutes. When the meat and potatoes are tender, the dish is ready.

Stinco di maiale al forno
Roast shank of pork

Servings 4
*Difficulty **Medium***
*Region **Trentino***
Alto Adige

Meat

4 pork shanks – 3½ tablespoons (5 cl) olive oil – 3½ oz (100 g) lard – ⅞ cup (2 dl) dry white wine – 2 cloves of garlic – 1 onion – 1 sprig of rosemary – salt – pepper – 4¼ cups (1 l) broth.

30 minutes preparation time + 3 hours minutes cooking time

Arrange the shins in an oven-dish with the lard, oil, the halved onion, the whole cloves of garlic and the rosemary. Turn the shins over to coat them well in fat and put the oven-dish into a hot oven at 400°F (200°C).
Brown the shins all over and then pour in the white wine. When it has evaporated, continue cooking adding stock or water.
The shins must never be allowed to remain dry. Cook until tender. Serve hot, accompanied by roast potatoes or salad.

Tomaxelle
Stuffed veal rolls

Servings 4
Difficulty Medium
Region Liguria

Meat

8 slices of veal – 3½ oz (100 g) lean veal – 3½ oz (100 g) veal udder – ¾ oz (20 g) dried mushrooms –fresh breadcrumbs soaked in broth – 2 tablespoons of grated Parmesan – 1 bunch of parsley – 5 sage leaves – 5 marjoram leaves – 1 egg – milk – extra virgin olive oil – broth – salt – pepper.

40 minutes preparation time + 40 minutes cooking time

Soak the mushrooms in lukewarm water, and then wring out the water and chop them up together with the herbs which have been washed and dried. Add the soaked bread, the lean veal, fried in butter and minced, beforehand, the parboiled minced veal udder, the Parmesan and the beaten egg. Mix it all together with a little milk.

Pound the veal slices, put the stuffing, as prepared above, on top of them, roll them up and fix them with a cocktail stick. Fry the meat rolls in two tablespoonfuls of oil and a little butter. When they are browned, season with salt and pepper to taste, add a ladle of broth and cook with a lid over a low heat for 30 – 40 minutes. Serve lukewarm.

Tortino di patate
Potato patties

Servings 6
Difficulty Low
Region Campania

Meat

5⅓ oz (150 g) cooked ham, diced – 2¼ lb (1 kg) potatoes – 2 tablespoons parsley, chopped – 1¾ oz (100 g) grated Parmesan cheese – 3½ tablespoons (50 ml) extra virgin olive oil – 2½ oz (70 g) breadcrumbs – 2 eggs – 5 egg yolks – ⅓ cup (8 cl) whole milk – salt – pepper – nutmeg.

30 minutes preparation time + 20 minutes cooking time

Put the potatoes in cold salted water in a pan over a high flame and boil. When they are cooked, drain and peel the potatoes while still hot and mash them immediately with a potato masher. Add the diced ham, the parsley, the Parmesan cheese, the eggs and the milk to the mashed potato. Add salt and pepper and grate in some nutmeg.

Grease a 12 inch (30 cm) baking tin with high edges and sprinkle with breadcrumbs.

Transfer the potato mixture into the baking tin and spread it out evenly.

Sprinkle breadcrumbs over it, and bake in the oven at 200°C (390°F).

Remove from oven when the surface is crispy and golden.

Chef's tips
If possible, do not use new potatoes;
they contain a lot of water and,
for that reason, would not produce
good results.

Venosino
Lamb stew with egg topping

Servings 4
Difficulty Medium
Region Basilicata

Meat

1 ¾ lb (800 g) lean lamb – ½ cup (1 dl) extra virgin olive oil – 1 onion – 14 ⅛ oz (400 g) canned peeled tomatoes – 1 lb 1 ½ oz (500 g) cardoons – 8 eggs – 2 ¾ oz (80 g) grated Pecorino cheese – 2 tablespoons parsley – salt.

20 minutes preparation time + 40 minutes cooking time

Remove the external filaments from the cardoons, cut them up into pieces, wash them and boil them in salted water. Strain them and keep them warm. Chop up the onion à la julienne.
Chop up the lamb into bite-sized pieces. Heat the oil in a large pan and when it is hot add the onion and the lamb and fry gently. After about 10 minutes, add the peeled tomatoes, and when it is cooked after about 30 minutes (if it dries up too much add some hot water or broth) add the cardoons, and simmer so they gain the flavor of the meat. Salt to taste. In the meantime, whisk the egg with the cheese, parsley and a little salt.
Transfer the meat and the vegetables to a circular baking tin, cover with the egg mixture and bake in a moderate oven at 350°F (180°C). Wait for the egg to become firm before serving. The size of the baking tin determines the thickness of the sauce.

Vitello in fricandò
Braised veal

Servings 4
*Difficulty **Medium***
*Region **Lombardy***

Meat

1 ⅓ lb (600 g) veal flank – 1 ¾ oz (50 g) butter – 4 slices Parma ham – 3 ½ table-spoons (5 cl) dry white wine – 1 carrot – 2 small onions – 1 bunch of parsley – 4 leaves of celery – 4 cloves – salt – pepper – meat broth.

20 minutes preparation time + 50 minutes cooking time

Remove the fat from the ham and use it to lard the veal. Stick the cloves into the whole onions. Heat the butter over a high flame and then fry the chopped ham and the two whole onions.
Fry the mixture well, then add the veal and brown it all over; add the carrot in small pieces and the bunch of parsley tied up together with a few celery leaves. Pour the white wine over the meat, season with salt and pepper and put on the lid. Cook the veal over a low heat, turning it frequently.
If during cooking the meat becomes too dry, add a little stock. Cut the veal into thin slices, pour over the sauce and the sieved vegetables and serve.

Baccalà alla cappuccina
Capuchin salted cod

Servings 4
Difficulty Low
Region Friuli
Venezia Giulia

Fish

2¼ lb (1 kg) salted cod, soaked – ½ cup (1 dl) olive oil – 2⅛ oz (60 g) flour – 1 white onion – 1¾ oz (50 g) pine nuts – 1¾ oz (50 g) raisins – 3 sardines, cleaned – 1 bay leaf – 1 lemon zest – 1 teaspoon sugar – 1 pinch cinnamon – ½ candied citron, thinly sliced – 1 teaspoon of grated bitter chocolate – pepper – 4¼ cups (1 l) broth – 1 cup (2 dl) white wine, boiling – breadcrumbs – salt.

20 minutes preparation time + 1 hour and 30 minutes cooking time

After soaking the salted cod, remove the skin and bones. Cut it into rather big chunks, flour well and sauté in a high-sided pot, arranging the pieces close to one another so that there are no gaps in between. Pour over some finely sliced sautéed onions. Add the bay leaf, sardines well cleaned and chopped, the pine nuts, raisins, lemon zest, the grated dark chocolate, salt and pepper.

Cover with boiling hot stock and cook over low heat for about three hours, without stirring but simply shaking the pot to prevent the fish from sticking to the bottom. If necessary, add more stock. Once the stock is absorbed, pour a glass of boiling hot wine over the cod. Finally, sprinkle with breadcrumbs and put in the oven at 350°F (180°C) until a golden crust forms on the surface. Serve piping hot with runny yellow polenta.

Baccalà alla vicentina
Stockfish Vicenza-style

Servings 4
Difficulty *Medium*
Region *Veneto*

Fish

1 lb 1⅝ oz (500 g) stockfish – 1 cup (250 ml) milk – 3½ oz (100 g) onion – ⅓ cup (8 cl) extra virgin olive oil – 1 oz (30 g) salted anchovies – ¼ oz (5 g) garlic – ⅓ oz (10 g) parsley – 2⅛ oz (60 g) all-purpose flour – grated Parmigiano Reggiano cheese to taste – salt – pepper.

30 minutes preparation time + 3 hours cooking time + 24 hours soaking time

Soak the stockfish for 24 hours. Remove the spinal bone and the other fish bones. Sauté the onion in a casserole in the oil over a medium heat, add a little salt and lower the heat. Add the crushed anchovies and chopped parsley.
Cut the stockfish into chunks, flour the chunks then sprinkle grated cheese on them.
Add a little milk to the casserole, keep on low heat, add stockfish and cook. Add more milk if necessary, season with a little salt and pepper and leave until the stockfish is cooked.

Chef's tips
Do not stir as the fish tends to come apart, simply jerk the casserole round gently with a circular movement.

300

Braciolette di pesce spada
Swordfish steaks

Servings 4
Difficulty Low
Region Sicily

Fish

1¾ lb (800 g) swordfish, thinly sliced – 5⅓ oz (150 g) breadcrumbs – 1 tablespoon capers – 1 oz (30 g) caciocavallo cheese, grated – 1 onion – pepper – parsley, chopped – olive oil – salt.

30 minutes preparation time + 10 minutes cooking time

Gently flatten out swordfish steaks using a meat mallet and cut into halves. Season breadcrumbs with salt, pepper and chopped parsley. Mix three quarters of the bread mixture with capers and grated *Caciocavallo* cheese, with a drop of oil; then spoon it onto the fish steaks.
Roll up the steaks and put onto a skewer alternated with pieces of onion (cleaned and cut into quarters). Coat the fish in oil and dip in the remaining breadcrumbs. Cook preferably over a charcoal grill, turning once only, or roast in a very hot oven for a few minutes. Serve hot.

Did you know that...
Swordfish was known and appreciated by the ancient Romans for its tenderness. Various documents from the 2nd century B.C. talk about fishing for swordfish around the Straits of Messina.

Calamari ripieni
Stuffed squid

Servings 4
Difficulty Medium
Region Apulia

Fish

4 medium sized squids – 5⅓ oz (150 g) breadcrumbs – 1 tablespoon parsley, chopped – 1 clove of garlic – 4¼ tablespoons (7 cl) tablespoons extra virgin olive oil – salt – pepper to taste.

20 minutes preparation time + 15 minutes cooking time

Clean the squids thoroughly inside, remove the heads and the tentacles and put to one side. Mince the heads and the tentacles and add the chopped garlic, the breadcrumbs, the parsley and the olive oil. Stuff the squid with this mixture, then place them in an oven dish with a drop of oil and a little water. Cook in the oven at 320°-340°F (160°-170°C) for 20 minutes. Then turn up the temperature to 400°F (200°C) to gratinate.

Cernia alla matalotta
Grouper matalotta-style

Servings 4
*Difficulty **Low***
*Region **Sicily***

Fish

1 ¾ lb (800 g) groupers – 2⅛ oz (60 g) flour – 7 oz (200 g) tomatoes – 3½ oz (100 g) onion – ¼ oz (5 g) garlic – 1 bay leaf – 1 oz (30 g) almonds – ⅓ oz (8 g) parsley – ½ cup (1 dl) white wine – 3½ tablespoons (5 cl) extra virgin olive oil – salt – pepper – ½ cup (1 dl) fish broth – 3½ oz (100 g) champignon mushrooms.
For the garnish: 3½ oz (100 g) zucchini – flaked almonds – 2²⁄₄ oz (80 g) mixed peppers.

25 minutes preparation time + 15 minutes cooking time

Place some flour in a tray with low edges and flour the grouper fillets.

Sauté the onion cut julienne-style and the thinly sliced garlic in oil for 1 minute.

Add fillets and fry gently. Add some white wine and simmer until it evaporates.

Add tomatoes cut into quarters, season with salt and pepper and add fish broth, bay leaf and mushrooms which have been cleaned and cut à la julienne.

Add chopped parsley and cook over low heat for 5 minutes.

Salt the remaining onion with sliced zucchini separately. Add peppers chopped into bits of approximately ⅔ inch (2 cm), add salt and sauté over a high flame. Finally, add the flaked almonds.

Arrange on a serving dish by placing the fillets first, then garnishing with the vegetables.

Filetto di scorfano all'acquapazza
Fillets of scorpion fish in "acqua pazza"

Servings 4
Difficulty Low
Region Campania

Fish

3²⁄₃ lb (1.2 kg) scorpion fish – 10½ oz (300 g) cherry tomatoes – 4¾ tablespoons (7 cl) extra virgin olive oil – 1 clove of garlic – 6 basil leaves – 5⅓ oz (150 g) onion – 1 pinch of fresh chili peppers – salt.

30 minutes preparation time + 15 minutes cooking time

Scale and gut the fish and cut into fillets. Cut the onion à la julienne and cut the garlic into slices. Wash the tomatoes and cut into quarters.
Soften the onion and garlic in the oil in a frying pan over a medium heat. Add the tomatoes, the basil and the chili pepper and cook until the tomatoes are soft.
Add the fillets, season with salt and pepper and add a drop of water (or if you have it, some cooking water from mussels or clams). Cook the fish and serve.

Chef's tips
It is advisable to cook the fish in the pan over a high flame so that the flesh does not absorb too much moisture.

Frittata con acciughe
Omelette with anchovies

Servings 4
Difficulty Low
Region Abruzzo

Fish

10 very fresh eggs – 6 desalted anchovies, ground in a mortar – 1 sprig parsley – 2 tablespoons (3 cl) oil – 1 clove of garlic, crushed – 10½ oz (300 g) tomato pulp – chili powder – salt.

10 minutes preparation time + 10 minutes cooking time

Heat the oil in a frying pan over a medium heat and when it is hot, fry the garlic until it is golden brown. Remove the garlic from the pan and add the anchovy paste, the parsley and the tomato. Add a little salt and the chili pepper powder and cook for 15 minutes.
Transfer the paste to a dish and leave to cool. Mix in the eggs with a pinch of salt and chili powder. Heat a drop of oil in a frying pan over a medium flame and when it is hot, pour in the omelette mixture. Stir for a few seconds and then leave to cook until it browns on one side. Turn the omelette out onto a large round plate. Heat the rest of the oil in the frying pan and cook the omelette on the other side. When it is cooked, slide the omelette onto a round serving dish and serve immediately.

Insalata di sgombro
Mackerel salad

Servings 4
Difficulty *Low*

Fish

4 mackerels, fresh, about 8¾ oz (250 g) each – 3½ oz (100 g) lettuce – 3½ oz (100 g) radicchio – 1¾ oz (50 g) raisins – 1¾ oz (50 g) pine nuts, roasted – 1 sprig parsley – 1 sprig chives – 6 mint leaves – 2¾ tablespoons (4 cl) extra virgin olive oil – sea salt with blood orange zest – 1⅓ tablespoons (2 cl) balsamic grape must – 3½ oz (100 g) Belice Olives.
For the vinegar court bouillon: 1¾ tablespoons (2.5 cl) vinegar – 1 carrot – 1 onion – 1 stalk celery – 5 whole peppercorns – 1 bay leaf – 8½ cups (2 l) water.
15 minutes preparation time + 1 hour and 45 minutes cooking time

Prepare the "court bouillon": boil all the chopped vegetables in the water and vinegar for 30 minutes. In the meantime, gut the mackerel, rinsing well under running water.
Wash the lettuce and the radicchio; soak the raisins in water. Cut the olives in half.
Boil the mackerel in the "court bouillon" for 10-15 minutes (depending on the size).
Strain and leave to cool. Separate the fillets and remove the bones in order to obtain 4 pieces from each fillet. Break up the lettuce and radicchio leaves with your hands; add chopped parsley, mint and chives and mix. Dress the salad with balsamic grape must and the sea salt with orange and toss. Add a little extra virgin olive oil at the end.
Arrange the salad on a serving dish; add the olives, raisins, pine nuts and lastly the mackerel fillets. Finish off the dish with more extra virgin olive oil and and grind a little pepper over it.

Pesce spada con capperi e limone
Swordfish with capers and lemon

Servings 4
Difficulty *Low*
Region *Calabria*

Fish

1 ¾ lb (800 g) swordfish cut into 4 slices – 2 cloves of garlic – 1 ¾ oz (50 g) capers, in vinegar – 1 bunch of parsley – 1 pinch of oregano – 1 lemon – 2 tablespoons (3 cl) extra virgin olive oil – salt.

20 minutes preparation time + 5 minutes cooking time

Heat the oil over a medium flame and sauté the whole cloves of garlic. Then gently fry the fish seasoned with salt and pepper. Then add the desalted roughly chopped capers.
When the fish has been sautéed on both sides, pour in the lemon juice and reduce. Add the chopped oregano and parsley and serve.

Did you know that...
Swordfish is a prized ingredient from the culinary traditions of Sicily and Calabria. It is used in the most refined recipes and it is extremely versatile; it can be easily accompanied with other characteristic products of the Mediterranean region, such as capers, lemon, eggplants, mint and peppers.

Polpettone di tonno
Tuna loaf

Servings 4
Difficulty **Medium**
Region **Marche**

Fish

14⅛ oz (400 g) canned tuna, in oil – 2 eggs – salt – ⅔ tablespoons (1 cl) olive oil –
parsley – 4 tablespoons Parmesan cheese, grated – zest of 1 lemon, grated.
15 minutes preparation time + 20 minutes cooking time

Drain the oil from the tuna and break into small pieces. Beat the eggs, add the tuna and a little parsley, cheese, breadcrumbs and lemon. Mix everything together and form into a loaf.
Meanwhile, take a sheet of parchment paper, grease with the oil and lay the loaf on top. Tie with
kitchen string.
Heat a large pot of water over a high flame and when starts to boil, immerse the loaf in the water
and leave to cook for about 20 minutes.
Drain, remove the paper, and leave to cool.
When the loaf is cold, cut it into slices. It can be served with a sauce made by blending extra virgin
olive oil, parsley, 2-3 cloves of garlic, an anchovy, a few capers and the juice of half a lemon.

Polpi in Purgatorio
Spicy stewed octopus

Servings 4
Difficulty Low
Region Molise

Fish

1 lb 1⅝ oz (500 g) baby octopuses – ¼ cup (6 cl) extra virgin olive oil – 2 onions – red chilli pepper – 1½ oz (40 g) parsley – salt and pepper.

30 minutes preparation time + 2 hours cooking time

Clean the octopuses in salted water and rinse well. Sauté the finely chopped onion and the chilli in a pan with the oil. Then add the octopuses, parsley, and a pinch of salt and pepper. Cover the pan with a lid and cook over a low heat for 2 hours, stirring the octopus from time to time with a wooden spoon.
Add a little water and cook until it evaporates. Serve warm.

Did you know that...
The red or spicy chilli pepper is an essential ingredient in this dish: polpi in purgatorio (or "octopuses in purgatory"). Originally from America, chilli peppers have been grown since 5500 B.C. They were brought to Europe by Christopher Columbus, who described them in his diary as "better in taste and nature than ordinary peppers." The chilli pepper had immediate success in the Old World, especially among the poorer classes of the population thanks to their strong flavor and low cost due to their adaptability and the fact that they were easy to grow. Because the wealthy did not appreciate their spicy flavor, the chilli pepper soon gained the nickname "the drug of the poor," who used them in large quantities to give flavor to their bland foods

Polpo alla Luciana
Octopus Luciana-style

Servings 4
Difficulty *Low*
Region **Campania**

Fish

1 ¾ lb (800 g) octopus – ½ cup (1 dl) extra virgin olive oil – 1 clove of garlic – 1 sprig of parsley – salt – pepper.

10 minutes preparation time + 2 hours cooking time

Clean the octopus, removing the beak and the eyes, then put it in a terracotta casserole that it just fits in. Add salt and pepper to taste and pour oil over it.

Seal the casserole with two sheets of straw paper, attaching them right round the vessel, put the lid on top and cook over a very low heat for about 2 hours, shaking the vessel every now and again to avoid the contents sticking to the bottom of the casserole.

Towards the end, remove the paper and continue cooking for another few minutes. Finally add the chopped parsley and garlic. Serve hot.

Rana pescatrice in brodetto di porri e olive nostrane
Monkfish in leek sauce with Italian olives

Servings 4
Difficulty *Low*
Region *Apulia*

Fish

3⅓ lb (1.5 kg) monkfish – 4¾ tablespoons (7 cl) extra virgin olive oil – 7 oz (200 g) ripe tomatoes – 1 lb 1⅝ oz (500 g) leeks – 2 cloves of garlic – 1 bunch of parsley – 1 lb 1⅝ oz (500 g) olives – 3 cups (7 dl) water – 1⅓ tablespoons (2 cl) white vinegar – chili pepper – salt – pepper.

40 minutes preparation time + 25 minutes cooking time

Remove the head, skin and tail from the monkfish and wash carefully.
Using a sharp knife, fillet the fish and remove the central bone to obtain 2 fillets.
Clean the leeks, remove the green part and slice the rest into round slices and then wash well under running water.
Blanch the leeks in water and vinegar, for a few seconds, drain and dry.
Cut the monkfish fillets into uniform pieces, blanch for a few minutes in abundant salted water. Drain and put to one side. Soften the leeks and the slivers of garlic in the oil over a medium heat, add a pinch of chili, the halved tomatoes, the parsley, and bring to the boil. Add the pieces of monkfish and the olives. Leave to cook over a low heat for 15 minutes. After seasoning with salt, and before serving, sprinkle with a little freshly ground pepper.

Sarde a beccafico
Stuffed sardines

Servings 4
Difficulty Medium
Region Sicily

Fish

3 ½ oz (100 g) toasted fresh breadcrumbs – 1 ¾ lb (800 g) sardines – 1 ⅓ tablespoons (2 cl) extra virgin olive oil – juice of ½ lemon – ⅓ oz (10 g) sugar – salt – pepper – 4 salted anchovies – 1 bunch of parsley – 1 ¾ oz (50 g) capers – 1 ¾ oz (50 g) stoned black olives, finely chopped – 1 ½ oz (40 g) sultanas – 1 ½ oz (40 g) pine nuts – 50 toasted almonds, finely crushed.
Some people also add: 1 clove of garlic, chopped – 1 shallot or onion, finely chopped – 2 ½ oz (60 g) grated Pecorino.

40 minutes preparation time + 15 minutes cooking time

Scale the sardines, remove the insides, the heads and the bones and wash them thoroughly.
Prepare the filling by mixing all the above ingredients.
For the filling: toast the breadcrumbs in a pan with a drop of extra virgin olive oil. Add the capers, the anchovies, the pine nuts, the almonds toasted beforehand in a frying pan, the olives, the parsley, the lemon zest, all chopped, the rest of the oil, the lemon juice and the sugar.
Variation 1: Add the chopped garlic, the finely chopped shallot or onion and the grated Pecorino cheese. When the filling is thoroughly mixed and smooth, spread a little on the sardines which should be open like a book. Close the sardines and press gently with your fingers.
Next, the sardines should be curled into a ring so that the tails point upwards, being careful to ensure that the filling does not come out. The sardines are then placed in a greased oven dish using laurel leaves to separate them.
Pour over some olive oil, sprinkle breadcrumbs over them and put in a very hot oven at 430°F (220°C) for 15-20 minutes.
Variation 2: In central and eastern Sicily, the sardines are stuffed as described above, and are then paired up, and placed one on top of the other and tied with kitchen string. They are then dipped in egg and breadcrumbs and fried in plenty of oil.

Seppie ripiene
Stuffed cuttlefish

Servings 4
Difficulty Low
Region Apulia

Fish

1 ¾ lb (800 g) cuttlefish – 7 oz (200 g) breadcrumbs – 1 ¾ oz (50 g) grated Pecorino cheese – 2 eggs – 1 clove of garlic – 1 tablespoon parsley, chopped – 1 ¾ (50 g) oz salted capers – ⅓ cup (8 cl) extra virgin olive oil – 2 ¾ oz (80 g) black olives – ⅞ cup (2 dl) white wine – salt – pepper.

40 minutes preparation time + 15 minutes cooking time

Clean the cuttlefish, without tearing them in half. Remove the bone, the ink sack and the insides, the skin and the eyes. Wash well under running water and drain. In the meantime, prepare the stuffing. Finely chop the cuttlefish tentacles, peeled garlic, parsley and the capers which have been desalted under running water. Beat the eggs in a bowl with the Pecorino cheese, salt and pepper. Add the breadcrumbs and the previously chopped ingredients.

Mix well to obtain a smooth mixture, then use to stuff the cuttlefish and close with a toothpick.

Place the cuttlefish in an oven-dish greased with oil, splash with wine and bake at 200°C (400°F) for about 30 minutes and leave to gratinate slightly.

Remove from the oven and leave to cool for a few minutes before serving.

Did you know that...
Stuffed cuttlefish were known and loved in ancient Rome and a recipe for the dish appears in the most important culinary text of the time, De re coquinaria *by Apicius, and more precisely in the 9th book.*

Seppioline su letto di polenta con salsa al nero
Baby cuttlefish on a bed of polenta with black sauce

Servings 4
Difficulty Low
Region Veneto

Fish

1 ⅓ lb (600 g) baby cuttlefish – 8¾ oz (250 g) fresh tomatoes – 4¾ tablespoons (7 cl) extra virgin olive oil – 1 bunch of parsley – 1 clove of garlic – ⅛ (4 g) cuttlefish ink – ½ cup (1 dl) white wine – ½ oz (5 g) salt – ¼ cup (8 cl) fish broth.
For the polenta: 8¾ oz (250 g) cornmeal – 4¼ cups (1 l) water.

40 minutes preparation time+ 15 minutes cooking time

Heat the oil in a frying pan over a medium heat, add the halved clove of garlic and the cuttlefish.

Sauté the cuttlefish for 1 minute, splash with white wine and evaporate. Season with salt and pepper.

Add diced tomato, pour in the fish stock and cook for about 3 minutes to evaporate. Add the parsley and the cuttlefish ink and cook till ready.

Bring a pan of water to boil. Add salt and slowly sprinkle in the cornmeal, stirring with a whisk. Cook for approximately 45 minutes.

Spoon a bed of soft polenta onto a serving dish, then pour in the cuttlefish into the center with the cuttlefish ink sauce.

Chef's tips
The cuttlefish ink must be added to the sauce at the end, as it tends to coagulate when exposed to too much heat.

Sformato di scampi e porcini
Scampi and porcini mushroom soufflé

Servings 4
Difficulty **Medium**
Region Veneto

Fish

10½ oz (300 g) scampi, peeled – 10½ oz (300 g) Porcini mushrooms – 1¾ oz (50 g) butter – 3½ tablespoons (5 cl) extra virgin olive oil – ½ cup (1 dl) white wine – 2¾ tablespoons (4 cl) Cognac liqueur – 2 cloves of garlic – 1 bunch of parsley – 1 egg yolk – 1 oz (30 g) cream – 3½ oz (100 g) grated Parmesan cheese – nutmeg – salt – pepper.
For the Sauce: 1¾ oz (50 g) all-purpose flour – 1¾ oz (50 g) butter – 4¼ cups (1 l) milk – 3½ oz (100 g) grated Parmesan cheese – salt – pepper.

45 minutes preparation time + 20 minutes cooking time

To make the sauce: melt the butter in a pan over medium heat, stir the flour into the butter and add the milk, a little at a time, stirring continuously with a whisk. Bring to the boil. Remove from the heat and add the Parmesan and continue to stir until it has completely dissolved.

To prepare the scampi: sauté the garlic in the butter over a medium heat and remove when golden. Put the scampi into the pan, add the wine and evaporate. Add a pinch of nutmeg, salt, pepper and the Cognac. To prepare the mushrooms: clean the mushrooms and cut into thin slices. Sauté the sliced mushrooms in the oil over a medium heat with salt and pepper. Add a chopped clove of garlic and the chopped parsley when they are cooked.

Mix together the scampi, mushrooms, sauce, the egg yolk, cream and grated Parmesan cheese.

Divide the mixture between individual greased ramekins or small molds. Bake in the oven for about 20 minutes at 360°F (180°C).

Stoccafisso con il pomodoro alla triestina
Stockfish with tomato sauce

Servings 4
Difficulty Medium
Region Friuli
Venezia Giulia

Fish

½ cup (1 dl) olive oil – 1¾ lb (800 g) stockfish – water – 1⅓ lb (600 g) tomatoes – 2 cloves of garlic – 1 bay leaf – salt – pepper.

20 minutes preparation time + 2 hours minutes cooking time + 24 hours soaking time

Pour the olive oil into an oven pot and then put in the stockfish, which has been soaked in water for 24 hours and cut into pieces. Cook with the lid on, over a moderate heat. Season with salt. If the cod sticks to the bottom of the pot, add a little water.

After an hour or so, add the blanched, peeled and chopped tomatoes, two garlic cloves, peeled and crushed, a bay leaf, pepper and a splash of oil.

Cover with water, put on the lid and cook in the oven for another hour at a medium temperature. Add another pinch of salt and serve with yellow polenta.

Tonno con caponata
Tuna steak with caponata

Servings 4
Difficulty Medium

Fish

1 lb (450 g) tuna – 3 ½ oz (100 g) onion – 3 ½ oz (100 g) eggplant – 3 ½ oz (100 g) zucchini – 3 ½ oz (100 g) red pepper – 1 oz (30 g) raisins – 1 oz (30 g) pine nuts – 1 oz (30 g) pistachios – 1 tablespoon white balsamic vinegar – 1 oz (30 g) sugar – 1 clove of garlic – 1 pinch salt – black pepper to taste – extra virgin olive oil to taste.

30 minutes preparation time + 15 minutes cooking time

In traditional "Caponata", the eggplants are fried first to give the dish more flavor.
The fried eggplant cubes are added to the other ingredients only at the end.
Pour a little extra virgin olive oil in a frying pan and sauté the finely chopped red onion first, then the red pepper and, at lastly, the diced zucchini.
After a 3 or 4 minutes minutes, add the other ingredients: capers, raisins, pine nuts, sugar, white vinegar, pistachios, and lastly the fried eggplant. Season with salt and pepper.
Once the caponata is ready, leave it to rest in a warm place, and prepare the tuna steak.
The tuna steak should be at least 1 inch (2.5 cm) thick so that it can be correctly seared.
First of all, season the steak with salt and pepper.
Heat a little extra virgin olive oil and the crushed garlic (to be removed later) in a frying pan over a medium heat and, when it is hot, sear the slice of tuna for about 1 minute on each side.
When the tuna steak has been seared, it can be served whole or cut into slices.

Did you know that...
In Sicily there are over 30 "traditional" versions of caponata?

Trota alla piemontese
Trout Piedmont-style

Servings 4
Difficulty Low
Region Piedmont

Fish

1 ¾ lb (800 g) trout – 1 ½ oz (40 g) raisins – 1 ¾ oz (50 g) onion – 1 ¾ oz (50 g) celery – ¼ oz (7 g) sage – ½ oz (14 g) garlic – ¼ oz (7 g) rosemary – 1 ¼ cups (300g) fish broth (court bouillon) – ⅔ tablespoons (10 ml) white wine vinegar – 2 ¾ tablespoons (40 ml) extra virgin olive oil – flour – salt – pepper.
For the garnish: 2 ¾ tablespoons (40 ml) extra virgin olive oil – 1 ½ oz (40 g) celery – 1 ½ oz (40 g) carrots – 1 ½ oz (40 g) zucchini – 1 teaspoon (5 g) balsamic vinegar – ¼ oz (7 g) thyme – ¼ oz (7 g) coriander.

20 minutes preparation time + 15 minutes cooking time

Chop the celery, onion, sage, rosemary, garlic finely and put in a skillet with the oil.
Place the fillets of fish on top of the vegetables and add the vinegar.
Spoon the broth onto the fish, add the raisins which have been soaked in water.
Adjust the salt and cook until the fish is done.
For the garnish, cut the zucchini, carrots and celery, into strips and sauté in the oil over a high flame.
Pour the balsamic vinegar onto the vegetables, add the coriander and thyme.
Arrange a bed of sautéed vegetables on a serving dish and place the trout fillets on top.

Chef's tips
Fillet the fish and remove
all the bones. While cooking,
do not turn the fish over
as it might break.

SIDE DISHES

SIDE DISHES

SIDE DISHES

MAIN COURSES ARE ACCOMPANIED BY A VARIETY OF SIDE-DISHES WHICH RANGE FROM THE SIMPLEST TO THE MOST COMPLICATED, CAPABLE OF BRINGING OUT THE BEST IN THE MAIN DISHES OF A MEAL WITH A TOUCH OF COLOR, TASTE AND IMAGINATION. THE MOST COMMON INGREDIENTS ARE UNDOUBTEDLY VEGETABLES, WHICH VARY FROM MONTH TO MONTH ACCORDING TO WHATEVER IS IN SEASON; BUT WE ALSO FIND THE UNMISTAKABLE AROMA OF MUSHROOMS AND PRIZED PULSES.

LEAFY VEGETABLES ARE PREPARED IN A SIMPLE MANNER AND ARE EATEN AS SALADS, WITH VARIOUS DRESSINGS AND FLAVORINGS, BUT THEY ARE ALSO COOKED IN WATER, OIL OR BUTTER AND USED TO FILL PIES AND QUICHES OR TO MAKE CREAMS AND PURÉES: SPINACH LENDS ITSELF VERY WELL TO A VARIETY OF PREPARATIONS, AS DO ENDIVES AND SOME TYPES OF CABBAGE.

SOME VEGETABLES LEND THEMSELVES TO FRYING IN BATTER OR IN BREADCRUMBS; POTATOES, ARTICHOKES, EGGPLANTS, ONIONS, CAULIFLOWERS... ALL BECOME A DELICIOUS ACCOMPANIMENT TO WHITE MEATS AND SOMETIMES ALSO TO FISH.

PULSES ARE PREPARED IN SOUPS AND PURÉES, AND ARE ALSO SERVED IN SALADS AFTER THOROUGH COOKING. ALL VEGETABLES CAN ALSO BE PRESERVED, IN OIL OR VINEGAR, AND ARE VERY TASTY WHEN SERVED WITH COLD CUTS AS WELL AS SALADS WITH VEGETABLES AND CEREALS OR FISH. SOME DISHES SUCH AS "CAPONATA" OR "CARPIONE" CAN BE REGARDED AS A MAIN COURSE IN THEIR OWN RIGHT. EVEN MUSHROOMS ARE OFTEN SERVED AS AN ACCOMPANIMENT, OR EVEN USED AS AN INGREDIENT IN EXQUISITE AND REFINED DISHES SUCH AS ESCALOPES... SOME TYPICAL RECIPES LIKE LENTILS, POTATO PURÉE, SAUERKRAUT, SPINACH COOKED IN BUTTER AND STEWED BEANS, ARE THE TYPICAL ACCOMPANIMENT TO GO WITH THE TRADITIONAL COOKED SAUSAGES OF EACH REGION. FRUIT VEGETABLES SUCH AS TOMATOES, EGGPLANTS, PEPPERS... CAN BE STUFFED AND COOKED IN THE OVEN, BUT CAN ALSO BE EATEN RAW WITH A FRESH SUMMERY STUFFING (ESPECIALLY TOMATOES). MANY VEGETABLES ARE SERVED RAW WITH LIGHT SUMMER DISHES: FOR EXAMPLE A RAW VEGETABLE DIP WITH A MEAT OR FISH CARPACCIO.

SIDE DISHES

SIDE DISHES

Fave al guanciale
Broad beans with pork cheek

Serving 4
Difficulty Low
Region Latium

Meat

2¼ lb (1 kg) broad beans (fava beans), fresh – 2⅔ oz (75 g) pork cheek – 1 small onion – 2 tablespoons (3 cl) extra virgin olive oil – salt – pepper.

30 minutes preparation time + 15 minutes cooking time

Shell and wash the broad beans under running water. Sauté the chopped onion and diced pork cheek in a pan (possibly earthenware), in the olive oil.

When the pork and the onion have colored slightly, add the fresh broad beans together with the salt and pepper, and cook for a while adding warm water from time to time, if necessary, and serve hot. If you use dried broad beans, which have already been boiled, reduce the cooking time and add a little dry white wine during cooking.

Insalata con speck
Radicchio with speck

Serving 4
Difficulty *Low*
Region *Trentino
Alto Adige*

Meat

2 heads red radicchio – 7 oz (200 g) speck (or smoked bacon) – 2 tablespoons (3 cl) balsamic vinegar – 2 tablespoons (3 cl) olive oil – salt.

15 minutes preparation time

Wash and dry the radicchio. Dice the speck or the bacon and sauté it in the oil in a pan. When the speck (or bacon) is golden brown, add the balsamic vinegar and let it evaporate. Use this sauce to dress red radicchio, seasoning with salt and pepper. Serve immediately.

Did you know that...
Speck is a type of uncooked seasoned ham that has been aged and lightly smoked. It is typical of the region of Alto Adige, and more specifically of the province of Bolzano. The meat has a characteristically bright pink color, with occasional veins of white fat. It is flat in shape and tastes of a harmonious mixture of salt, spices and smoke.

Torta rustica di carciofi
Country-style artichoke pie

Serving 4
Difficulty *Low*
Region *Abruzzo*

Meat

For pastry: 7 oz (200 g) all-purpose flour – 7 oz (200 g) ricotta cheese – ½ cup (1 dl) extra virgin olive oil.
For the filling: 12 artichokes – 2 small mozzarella cheeses – 8¾ oz (250 g) Parma ham – 1¾ oz (50 g) grated Pecorino cheese – 3 eggs – 3½ oz (100 g) Fontina cheese, very thinly sliced – salt.

40 minutes preparation time + 45 minutes cooking time

Prepare a very soft dough and divide it into two parts that will be used for the base and the top of the pie. Clean the artichokes by removing the external leaves, cut them in half and remove any internal fibers and then chop them up à la julienne. Sauté the artichokes in a frying pan over a medium heat with a little butter, salt and pepper. Dice the ham and the Mozzarella finely, put in a bowl and add the eggs mixed with grated Pecorino and the artichokes prepared beforehand.
Roll out the pastry dough and place one part on the bottom of an oven dish and then put the slices of Fontina on top. Add the filling and close the pie with the remaining part of the pastry.
Bake in a hot oven at 400°F (200°C) for about 45 minutes.

Asparagi di Bassano con salsa di uova sode
Asparagus with hard-boiled egg sauce

Serving 4
Difficulty Low
Region Veneto

Fish

2¼ lb (1 kg) asparagus (preferably the white kind from Bassano) – 3 eggs, hard-boiled – 2 anchovies, chopped – 1 tablespoon capers, chopped – the juice of 1 lemon – ½ cup (1 dl) extra virgin olive oil – salt – pepper.

15 minutes preparation time + 8 minutes cooking time

Clean the asparagus, tie it in bunches and stand upright in a tall, narrow pot. Add cold water until ⅔ of the stalks are covered and simmer for about 8 minutes.

In another pan hard-boil the eggs by leaving them to boil in salted water for 10 minutes after they begin to boil. Remove the shells from the hard boiled eggs, cut in half, remove the yolks from the whites and sieve the yolks. Add about two tablespoons of lemon juice to the egg yolks and very very slowly, stirring continuously, pour in as much olive oil as is necessary to obtain a rather liquid sauce. Chop up the whites and add half of them to the sauce. Also add the chopped capers and chopped anchovies and pepper and adjust the salt and lemon juice to taste.

The asparagus can be served very hot, to dip individually in the sauce on the plates. Alternatively you can leave them to cool and serve them on a plate with the sauce and garnish with the remaining chopped egg whites.

Carciofi alla Cavour
Artichokes Cavour

Serving 4
Difficulty Low
Region Piedmont

Fish

8 artichokes – 2 eggs, hard-boiled – 1 sprig parsley – 1 lemon – 2 anchovies – butter – grated Parmesan cheese.

20 minutes preparation time + 10 minutes cooking time

Select small very tender artichokes, clean and boil them in salted water with lemon juice.
Strain the artichokes and drizzle with melted butter, roll them in grated Parmesan cheese and then place them in an oven dish and cook in a hot oven at 400°F (200°C) for a few minutes.
Finely chop the peeled hard-boiled eggs with a tablespoon of parsley leaves and two anchovies, rinsed and boned beforehand. Heat 1¾ oz (50 g) of butter in a small saucepan and heat until it is foaming, then blend in the egg-anchovy-parsley mixture. Stir well and pour over the artichokes. Serve hot.

Did you know that...
The Count Camillo Benso di Cavour, the famous statesman who diplomatically engineered the unification of Italy, led a full life and enjoyed all of life's pleasures: love, good food, and travel throughout Europe, especially to London and Paris.

Fave alle acciughe
Broad beans with anchovies

Serving 4
Difficulty Low
Region Marches

Fish

2¼ lb (1 kg) broad beans, fresh (fava beans)- 2 cloves of garlic – 1 pinch marjoram – 4 anchovies – 4 tablespoons extra virgin olive oil – vinegar – salt – pepper.

10 minutes preparation time + 5 minutes cooking time

Boil the broad beans in a small quantity of salted water until they are cooked "al dente." Meanwhile, prepare a sauce with a mixture of the chopped anchovies, garlic, marjoram, vinegar, oil, salt and pepper. This will be used to dress the broad beans as soon as they have been drained.

There is a variant: Fresh broad beans blanched in boiling salted water and then seasoned with chopped garlic, oil, marjoram, salt and pepper.

Another sauce can be made using fresh chopped chives, olive oil, salt and pepper.

Peperoni ripieni
Stuffed peppers

Serving 4
Difficulty *Low*
Region *Piedmont*

Fish

4 peppers – 7 oz (200 g) mozzarella cheese – 5⅓ oz (150 g) ricotta cheese – 1 tablespoon Parmesan cheese – 3½ oz (100 g) canned tuna, drained – 3 desalted and boned anchovies – 1 sprig of parsley – 5 sage leaves – 6 tablespoons tomato sauce with 1 teaspoon of sugar – 1 teaspoon red wine vinegar – 5 basil leaves, cut into pieces – 1 pinch oregano (or thyme) – 2 eggs, whole – 1 egg yolk – breadcrumbs – salt.

15 minutes preparation time + 15 minutes cooking time

Place the washed peppers in an oven dish and cook in the oven at 350°F (180°C). After about 30 minutes remove them from the oven, peel them, remove the seeds and cut them up into approximately 1⅔ inches (4 cm) wide lozenge shapes.

For the stuffing, dice all the cheese finely, crumble the tuna fish, chop the anchovies with parsley and sage, cut the basil à la julienne. Mix all the ingredients well in a bowl together with the vinegar, the whole eggs and the egg yolk, the oregano, the Parmesan cheese the tomato sauce and the breadcrumbs. When the stuffing is thoroughly mixed, put a spoonful on each of the pepper lozenge shapes and roll them up. Put the stuffed peppers in an oven dish and cook in a hot oven at 400°F (200°C) with a little oil and water. Serve hot or warm.

Peperoni ripieni alla siciliana
Stuffed peppers Sicilian-style

Serving 4
Difficulty Low
Region Sicily

Fish

4 peppers – 8½ oz (240 g) breadcrumbs – 4 tomatoes – 4 salted anchovies – 2 tablespoons of capers – 1¾ oz (50 g) Caciocavallo cheese, grated – extra virgin olive oil – basil – salt – pepper.

30 minutes preparation time + 25 minutes cooking time time

Using the tip of a knife, remove the stalk and the seeds of the peppers, taking care not to break them. Then cut them in half. Brown the breadcrumbs lightly in a pan and season with salt, pepper and plenty of basil. Add the grated Caciocavallo cheese, the capers, the tomatoes and the anchovies cut into small pieces. Mix well, adding a little oil and stuff the peppers with the mixture.
Place the peppers in a greased oven dish, add a little oil, cover with aluminum foil and cook in the oven at 400°F (200°C) for 15 minutes first, and then remove the aluminum foil and cook for another 10 minutes adding (if necessary) a little oil. Serve lukewarm or even cold.

Did you know that...
Peppers originated in South America, and are a closely related to chili peppers even though they are not spicy.

Cipolle ripiene
Stuffed onions

Serving 4
*Difficulty **Low***
*Region **Piedmont***

Vegetable

3⅓ lb (1.5 kg) onion – 1 bunch herbs – 3½ oz (100 g) butter – 7 oz (200 g) bread-crumbs – ½ cup (1 dl) milk – 1 oz (30 g) raisins – 4 eggs – 7 oz (200 g) grated Parmesan cheese.

40 minutes preparation time + 15 minutes cooking time

Boil the onions (preferably the flat white summer variety, Borretta), cut them horizontally and empty them. Finely chop various herbs (parsley, sage, rosemary, thyme, basil, mint, rucola, celery leaves or others of your choice) together with the pulp from inside the boiled onions.
Sauté in butter and salt to taste. Meanwhile soak the breadcrumbs in the milk and soften the raisins in warm water. Mix the herbs and the chopped onions with the bread and raisins, together with 2 eggs and a little grated Parmesan cheese.
Stuff the boiled onions with the mixture and arrange them in an oven-dish.
Meanwhile, beat 2 eggs with 5⅓ oz (150 g) of grated Parmesan cheese, adding a little milk.
Pour the mixture over the onions almost covering them. Put a flake of butter on top of each onion.
Bake in a moderate oven at 350°F (180°C) until the surface is golden brown.

Did you know that...
Onions probably originated in central Asia where they have been grown for over 5000 years. They were defined by the famous French gourmet, Brillat-Savarin, as "the people's truffles." Onions were an important ingredient in the cuisine of all principal populations of the Mediterranean in Ancient times.

Insalata di lampascioni
Lampascioni salad

Serving 4
Difficulty Low
Region Basilicata

Vegetable

1 lb 1⅝ oz (500 g) lampascioni (*Muscari comosum*, or grape hyacinth, bulbs that are also known as wild onions) – 2¾ tablespoons (4 cl) extra virgin olive oil – 1⅓ tablespoons (2 cl) white wine vinegar – 1 sprig of parsley – salt – pepper.

15 minutes preparation time + 24 hours soaking

Clean the "lampascioni" by removing the outer leaves, wash well and leave in cold water for a day, changing the water often.
Then boil them and let them to cool down in the cooking liquid. Strain and season with salt, pepper, vinegar, olive oil and parsley. Mix well and serve.

Insalata di Natale
Christmas salad

Serving 4
*Difficulty **Low***
*Region **Sicily***

Vegetable

10½ oz (300 g) chicory, sweet – 10½ oz (300 g) celery – 2 tablespoons capers in brine – 2 tablespoons green olives – 1 orange – 1 lemon – 1 pomegranate – 2 tablespoons (3 cl) extra virgin olive oil – salt.

25 minutes preparation time

Boil the chicory and celery separately. Drain and leave to cool. Then mix and add the olive oil.
Add well-rinsed capers and the chopped olives. Mix well and arrange on a serving dish.
Place orange and lemon slices without the skin on top of your Christmas salad, then cover with pomegranate seeds.

Insalata di olive verdi schiacciate
Green olive salad

Serving 4
Difficulty Low
Region Sicily

Vegetable

14⅛ oz (400 g) Sicilian olives from Belice – 3½ oz (100 g) celery – 1⅓ tablespoons (2 cl) extra virgin olive oil – 5 mint leaves – ⅔ tablespoons (1 cl) white wine vinegar – salt – chili (optional).

15 minutes preparation time

Crush the pitted olives, and rinse under running water.
Put them into a salad bowl, add the celery and mint leaves and dress with oil, abundant vinegar and salt. As an option, you can also add a hot chili pepper cut into small pieces.

Did you know that...
Both the Greeks and the Romans, believed the olive tree gave strength and purified the body, but it was also a sign of peace and prosperity. It was so precious that it was considered a gift of the gods.

Insalata di pompelmo rosa, spinaci novelli e noci
Salad with pink grapefruit, young spinach and walnuts

Serving 4
Difficulty *Low*
Region *Emilia Romagna*

Vegetable

2 pink grapefruits – 16 walnuts – 7 oz (200 g) young spinach leaves, fresh – 3 ½ tablespoons (5 cl) extra virgin olive oil – salt – pepper.

10 minutes preparation time

Peel the grapefruit and divide into segments. Squeeze the remaining pulp into a container, add the salt and extra virgin olive oil to the orange to obtain a citronette dressing. Wash and dry the spinach carefully. Shell the walnuts. Add the citronette dressing to the spinach in a bowl.
Arrange the salad on a plate and garnish with the walnuts and grapefruit segments.
Before serving, sprinkle with ground black pepper.

Did you know that...
Among the ingredients of this unusual spring salad are walnuts. Since ancient times they have been a symbol of life.
In Roman times they used to be thrown at the bride and groom because their sound covered the shouts of the bride during her simulated kidnapping. She then had to throw the walnuts because their falling and bouncing was a sign of good fortune.
Such traditions have not been completely lost in Europe although rice is now thrown at weddings in Italy.

Lampascioni fritti
Fried lampascioni

Serving 4
Difficulty Low
Region Basilicata

Vegetable

1⅔ lb (700 g) lampascione (*Muscari comosum*, or grape hyacinth, bulbs that are also known as wild onions) – 2 tablespoons (3 cl) extra virgin olive oil – 2¾ oz (80 g) breadcrumbs – salt – pepper – chili (optional).

20 minutes preparation time + 15 minutes cooking time + 24 hours soaking time

Peel and wash the "lampascioni." Leave them to soak in cold water for one or two days changing the water several times, or boil them in abundant water until they are half-cooked to remove the bitter taste.

Then sauté the garlic in the oil over a medium heat and add the properly dried "lampascioni." Salt, pepper and flavor to taste with chili pepper. Sauté the "lampascioni," pressing them down to cook them well inside. A few minutes before they are cooked, add the breadcrumbs and brown lightly.

Melanzane alla parmigiana
Eggplant with tomato and parmesan

Serving 4
*Difficulty **Medium***
*Region **Emilia Romagna***

Vegetable

14⅛ oz (400 g) eggplant – 3⅓ oz (100 g) butter – ½ cup (8 cl) extra virgin olive oil – 1 yellow onion – 3½ oz (100 g) tomato sauce – salt – black pepper – ½ cup (1 dl) vegetable broth – 3½ oz (100 g) Parmesan cheese.

30 minutes preparation time + 1 hour cooking time

Select good eggplants and cut them, vertically, into slices about ⅛ inch (3 mm) thick and boil in plenty of water for five minutes Drain and leave to dry between two kitchen cloths.
Place a medium casserole with the butter and olive oil over a medium heat, and when the butter is melted, add the chopped onion.
Add the tomato sauce and the thoroughly dried eggplants, cook for thirty minutes, stirring every so often, and adding a little broth if needed. Cook until the eggplants are soft and completely cooked. You can serve immediately or at room temperature after a few hours, after adding a little Parmesan cheese.

Did you know that...
The term "parmigiana" (or in the style of Parma) is not only used for traditional recipes from Parma. Between the 17th and 19th centuries, this word was used to describe any recipe with Parmesan cheese and, more generally, for vegetable dishes layered with other ingredients.

Pinzimonio
Raw vegetable dips

Serving 4
*Difficulty **Low***

Vegetable

1 cucumber – 1 fennel bulb – 8 radishes – 2 carrots – 2 stalks of celery – 1 red pepper – 2 endives – extra virgin olive oil – balsamic vinegar – sea salt with orange zest.

15 minutes preparation time

Wash and chop the carrots, the cucumber, the peppers into sticks and the fennel, the endive into longitudinal segments. Remove the roots and the leaves from the radishes leaving just half an inch of stalk from which they can be picked up between finger and thumb.

For the vinaigrette: add 1 tablespoon of balsamic vinegar per person, add a pinch of salt and stir well with a fork. Add the extra virgin olive oil with 3 parts of oil to 1 part of vinegar or up to 4 parts of oil to 1 part of vinegar, depending on taste. Pour the vinaigrette into small bowls to serve individually to each guest in which they can dip the vegetables before eating them.

Sformato di cavolo
Cabbage soufflé

Serving 4
Difficulty *Medium*
Region *Valle d'Aosta*

Vegetable

½ savoy cabbage – 1 onion – 1 bay leaf – 4 eggs – 3 egg yolks – 7 oz (200 g) cream – 1 small bunch of basil – 1 ¾ lb (800 g) Fontina cheese – as much milk as it takes to cover the diced Fontina cheese – salt – pepper.

40 minutes preparation time + 40 minutes cooking time

Stew the onion and shredded cabbage together with some bay leaves. Remove the bay leaves and chop in a blender adding the basil. Strain through a chinois strainer (conical strainer), add the eggs, and the cream and whisk well. Grease 4 molds with butter, pour in the mixture and cook, covered, in a bain-marie at 300-320°F (150-160°C) until firm. Prepare a tasty "fondue" and serve together with the flan. For the fondue, dice the Fontina, put into a casserole, cover with the milk, add a pinch of pepper, and cook in a bain-marie, mixing with a wooden spoon until a smooth mixture is obtained. At this point, add the three yolks to the Fontina cream, taking care to blend them in without cooking them. The Fontina cheese sauce can be poured over the soufflé or you can put a thin layer under the soufflé.

Did you know that...
People have eaten cabbage for centuries, dating back to Ancient Egypt.
In Ancient Greece, cabbage was considered sacred, while the Romans
thought it was a panacea for all ills that, when eaten raw before meals,
allowed you to drink as much wine as you wanted without getting drunk.

Torta di melanzane
Eggplant flan

Serving 4
Difficulty Low
Region Lombardy

Vegetable

4 eggplants – 2 eggs – 1¾ oz (50 g) breadcrumbs – 1¾ oz (50 g) grated Parmesan cheese – ¾ oz (20 g) butter, melted – nutmeg.

30 minutes preparation time + 20 minutes cooking time

Peel the eggplants and cut them in quarters, cook immediately in very little salted water, for 10 minutes. Drain and squeeze them tightly to remove all the cooking water and the bigger seeds. Put the eggplants in a bowl and mix in the egg yolks and whites, a generous spoonful of grated cheese and a tablespoon of bread crumbs.
Add the melted butter (melted but not fried) and a good sprinkling of grated nutmeg.
Mix well and place in an oven tin, buttered and coated in breadcrumbs. Bake in a hot oven at 320°F (160°C) for 20 minutes and serve piping hot.

Did you know that...
The Arabs were responsible for bringing the eggplant, or badingian in Arabic, to Europe. The vegetable did not catch on until after 1500 due to the fact that they were referred to as mela insana, or "insane apple" in Italian. For a long period, eggplants were thought to be bad for your health and were considered to be an immoral food because of its presumed aphrodisiac properties.

Zucchine in agrodolce
Sweet and sour zucchini

Serving 4
Difficulty *Low*
Region *Sardinia*

Vegetable

2¼ lb (1 kg) zucchini, small – ¼ cup (6 cl) wine vinegar – 2⅛ oz (60 g) granulated sugar – frying oil – salt.

15 minutes preparation time + 15 minutes cooking time

In a small frying pan over a low heat, dissolve the sugar in the vinegar and keep warm.
Wash the zucchini and cut into disks ¼ inch (½ cm) thick. Fry the zucchini, a few at a time, in oil over a high flame. Once they have been fried, arrange them in an oven dish. Add salt and pour over the sweet and sour marinade prepared beforehand. In summer these are also good served cold.

Did you know that...
Sweet and sour sauces can be traced back to the ancient use of mixing sweet ingredients with more acidic ones to create distinctive, intense flavors. Indeed, there are traces of "sweet and sour" flavors from Roman times when they were made by combining honey with vinegar.

SWEETS and FRUIT

SWEETS and FRUIT

Sweets in relation to a meal are like a "hat" in relation to an outfit; an unnecessary yet very pleasant accessory.

The aromas, the colors, the pleasant texture of a cream dessert, a slice of cake, a blancmange or a soft fritter, can all render the most frugal of meals special or put the perfect finishing touch to a sumptuous refined dinner.

There are sweets to suit all tastes, from *haute patisserie* to home made ones that are just as tasty and enjoyable; from spoon cream desserts to oven baked sweets and on to the traditional fried sweets with the most varied regional names.

Among the soft spoon sweets there are recipes for simple blancmanges, refined cream desserts, sumptuous bavarian creams and elaborate *charlottes*, *mont-blanc* domes, rich trifles, elegant *soufflés*, cute *zuccotti*, and homemade rice puddings ...

SPOON SWEETS ALSO INCLUDE ICE CREAM AND SORBETS MADE WITH DIFFERENT COMBINATIONS OF MILK, FRUIT, SUGAR AND EGGS TOGETHER WITH VARIOUS OTHER INGREDIENTS AND AROMAS. ICE CREAM IS LOVED BY EVERYBODY, ESPECIALLY CHILDREN, ABOVE ALL WHEN IT IS PREPARED IN A TRADITIONAL WAY OR EVEN AT HOME, THANKS TO TODAY'S MODERN ICE CREAM MAKING MACHINES.

THERE ARE MANY TYPES OF CAKES AND TARTS, RANGING FROM TARTS FILLED WITH HOME-MADE JAM, TO THOSE FILLED WITH CREAM, FRESH FRUIT IN SEASON, CHOCOLATE AND RICOTTA. LARGE RING SHAPED CAKES – CIAMBELLONI, APPLE CAKES, BREAD CAKES, CHOCOLATE CAKES, CORNMEAL CAKES AND RICE CAKES ARE ALL PART OF THE HOME-COOKING TRADITION.

FRIED SWEETS ARE TYPICAL OF THE CARNIVAL PERIOD, BUT IN SOME REGIONS THEY ARE ALSO MADE FOR CHRISTMAS AND EASTER: THE WELL KNOWN "FRAPPE," "CROSTOLI," "CENCI," ALL SORTS OF FRITTERS (RICE, AP-

PLE, SEMOLINA, ...), CREAM OR JAM FILLED TORTELLI, *KRAPFEN*, RING SHA-
PED COOKIES; THE WONDERFUL SICILIAN CANNOLI FILLED WITH FRESH RI-
COTTA AND CANDIED FRUIT.

SOME SWEETS ARE PREPARED WITH FRUIT SUCH AS FRUIT SALADS FLAVO-
RED WITH LEMON, ORANGE OR LIQUEURS, OTHERS ARE BAKED IN THE OVEN
LIKE STUFFED PEACHES, PEARS IN SWEET WINE OR CARAMELIZED APPLES;
OR FLAMBÉED, SERVED IN CARAMELIZED SALADS OR TOPPED WITH WHIP-
PED CREAM.

FOR IMPORTANT OCCASIONS THERE ARE THEN THE *PATISSERIE* CLASSICS
SUCH AS "MILLEFOGLIE," "PROFITEROLES," CHOCOLATE CAKES AND VA-
RIOUS CAKES SOAKED WITH LIQUEURS.

CRÊPES WITH JAM AND CREAM, SOMETIMES SPLASHED WITH LIQUEUR
AND *FLAMBÉED*, ARE A REFINED CLASSIC DESSERT TO ROUND UP A LIGHT
LUNCH.

SWEETS
AND FRUIT

Bianco mangiare
Bianco mangiare

Servings 4
*Difficulty **Low***

Sweet

8¼ oz (250 g) almonds – 7 oz (200 g) sugar – 4 sheets of gelatine.

20 minutes preparation time + 6 h refrigeration time

Finely grind the peeled almonds using a mortar and pestle or a food processor, gradually adding a little water to form a paste. Mix together well then wrap the paste in a kitchen towel. Place the towel resting over a bowl and squeeze out any excess water. Soak the gelatine in hot water for a few minutes and then wring out the water. Mix together the almond paste, sugar and sheets of gelatine. Transfer the mixture into a lightly greased rectangular mold and place in the refrigerator for at least 6 hours. Serve sliced.

Biscotti al cocco
Coconut cookies

Servings 4
Difficulty *Low*

Sweet

6 oz (170 g) coconut flour – 7 oz (200 g) granulated sugar – 1 ½ oz (40 g) flour –
2 eggs – 1 pinch salt – cocoa powder – icing sugar.
5 minutes preparation time + 10 minutes cooking time

Mix together the flours and sugar and form a well on a work surface. In the center, add the eggs and
the salt. Mix together until you have a smooth dough.
Then divide the dough into small balls, about ½ inch (1 cm) in diameter, and roll in either icing sugar or cocoa powder.
Arrange the cookies on a baking tin lined with parchment paper. Bake in the oven at 280°F (140°C)
oven for about 10 minutes.

Biscotti caserecci
Homemade cookies

Serving 20
Difficulty Medium
Region Apulia
Sweet

2¼ lb (1 kg) all-purpose flour – 1 lb 1⅝ oz (500 g) sugar – 4 eggs – 1 egg yolk – ¾ oz (20 g) Baker's ammonia (ammonium carbonate) – lemon zest, grated – milk – 1⅔ lb (700 g) almonds.

20 minutes preparation time + 30 minutes cooking time

Mix all the ingredients, adding milk if necessary, to make a soft mixture. Shape the mixture into a large sausage shape, brush with beaten egg yolk, then bake in a hot oven at 400°F (200°C). Halfway through the cooking, remove from the heat and cut into finger thick slices and then put the biscuit slices back into the oven to finish cooking.

Biscotti di Carnevale
Carnival cookies

Servings 4
Difficulty Low

Sweet

7 oz (200 g) flour – 1¾ oz (50 g) potato starch – 5½ oz (160 g) butter – 3½ oz (100 g) icing sugar – 1 egg yolk – ½ stick of vanilla.

40 minutes preparation time + 15 minutes cooking time

Begin by removing the butter from the refrigerator and leaving it at room temperature for at least 30 minutes, to soften.

Mix together the dry ingredients: flour, potato starch and the icing sugar. Then add the egg yolk, followed by the butter, working the dough gently with your hands until it well mixed, but without kneading the mixture excessively. Cover the dough in plastic wrap and leave in the refrigerator for at least 30 minutes. Then, roll out the dough, using a rolling pin, about ¼ inch (½ cm) thick. Cut out cookies from the dough and place on a baking tin lined with parchment paper.

Bake the cookies in a 350°F (180°C) oven for 13 to 15 minutes.

Biscotti di mandorla
Almond cookies

Serving 10
Difficulty *Medium*
Region *Abruzzo*

Sweet

3 eggs – 14⅛ oz (400 g) sugar – 8¾ oz (250 g) peeled almonds, whole – 1 small sachet of baking powder – 14⅛ oz (400 g) flour.

20 minutes preparation time + 30 minutes cooking time

Mix all the ingredients and form a log shape with the dough. Place it on a baking tin lined with parchment paper. Bake in the oven at 356°F (180°C) for about 30 minutes.
Cut the biscuits out of the dough and return to the oven for about 20 minutes for the second baking.

Bonet
Bonet (typical sweet from Piedmont)

Serving 10
Difficulty Low
Region Piedmont

Sweet

2⅛ cups (5 dl) whole milk, – 10½ oz (300 g) granulated sugar – 4¼ oz (120 g) amaretti biscuits – 2½ oz (70 g) cocoa powder – 3 eggs – 1 egg yolk – 1 teaspoon (5 g) rum.
For the caramel: 10½ oz (300 g) granulated sugar – ½ cup (1 dl) water.

15 minutes preparation time + 45 minutes cooking time

Put the sugar into a casserole and add the water, cook over a medium heat until the caramel becomes a deep brown color.

Pour the caramel into the molds for Bonet and leave to cool.

Put the whole eggs into a bowl and beat them together with the sugar. Blend in the cocoa powder and mix well. Add the crumbled amaretti biscuits and the rum. Heat the milk separately and then add it to the mixture, mixing continuously with a whisk. Pour the mixture into the caramel-coated molds.

Put the molds into a baking tray containing hot water and cook the Bonet bain-marie style in the oven at 300°F for 40'-50', until the dessert has completely solidified.

Chef's tips
Let it cool well before turning it out of the molds. It tastes better when eaten the following day.

Cancelle
Anise-flavored cakes

Serving 4
Difficulty *Medium*
Region *Molise*

Sweet

3 eggs – 2 tablespoons (30 g) extra virgin olive oil – 6 tablespoons sugar – 1⅓ tablespoons (20 g) anise liqueur or 1 glass of dry white wine – 1 lemon – 1 lb (450 g) flour – 1 pinch salt.

30 minutes preparation time + 5 minutes cooking time

Beat the eggs with the sugar in a bowl until they become fluffy, add the oil, the salt and the grated lemon zest. Mix all the ingredients together thoroughly and add as much flour as the mixture will absorb. The mixture must become firm like the dough for "gnocchi."

Flavor the mixture with the anise and turn it onto a pastry board coated in flour. Keep kneading until it becomes smooth, and then cut into pieces. Roll these out one at a time on the pastry board and form small balls, the size of a walnut.

When all the dough has been used up, grease the two plates of the special iron griddle used to make "Cancelle," heat over the hob and as soon as it is hot enough, place a ball of dough in the center, close the griddle, and put back over the heat for a few minutes, turning to heat both sides until the "Cancella" is golden and crunchy.

Canederli di albicocche
Apricot dumplings

Serving 4
*Difficulty **Medium***
*Region **Trentino Alto Adige***

Sweet

2¼ lb (1 kg) potatoes (floury)- 8¾ oz (250 g) all-purpose flour – 3 eggs – 7 oz (200 g) butter – 3½ oz (100 g) breadcrumbs – salt – 3½ oz (100 g) sugar – cinnamon powder – 16 apricots, pitted.

30 minutes preparation time + 5 minutes cooking time

Boil the potatoes, then peel them and mash with a ricer on a pastry board. Leave to cool, then add the sieved flour, the eggs, and a curl of butter. Salt and mix well using your hands.

Form the dough into a salami shape, then divide it into pieces about 6 inches (15 cm) long. Squash the pieces of dough into squares big enough to enclose an apricot. Wrap the apricot in the dough, with floured hands, to form a ball.

Bring abundant salted water to the boil and toss in the "canederli" and wait for them to float to the surface, then strain. Meanwhile, in a pan melt the butter. When it becomes golden, add the breadcrumbs, stir and after a minute or two pour in the "canederli," stirring them with a wooden spoon to flavor them uniformly. Serve hot, dusted with sugar and cinnamon.

Cannoli siciliani
Sicilian cannoli

Serving 10
*Difficulty **Low***
*Region **Sicily***

Sweet

For the shells: 7 oz (200 g) all-purpose flour – 1 oz (30 g) cocoa powder – ⁷⁄₈ oz (25 g) sugar – 2 eggs – ¾ oz (20 g) butter – salt – 1 tablespoon Marsala wine, or Rum
For the filling: – 2¼ lb (1 kg) ricotta cheese, sweet – 1 lb 1½ oz (500 g) sugar – milk – vanilla – cinnamon – 3½ oz (100 g) mixed candied fruit, diced – 3½ oz (100 g) dark chocolate, chopped.
Garnish: pistachio, ground – very fine icing sugar.

30 minutes preparation time + 2 minutes cooking time + 30 minutes resting time

To make the crispy shells, mix together the flour, cocoa powder, melted butter and eggs in a bowl. Then add the Marsala, or if you prefer, the rum. Continue mixing until the dough is smooth, then wrap it in plastic wrap and let it rest for half an hour.

Roll out the cannoli dough and cut it into approximately 4 inch (10 cm) squares. Then wrap the squares around the metal tubes to shape the cannoli. Fry the dough, still wrapped around the tubes, in abundant boiling lard or olive oil. Leave the cannoli to cool on paper towels. Once cool, slide out the metal tubes. To make the ricotta-based filling, beat the ricotta and sugar with a fork, adding a drop of milk and a dash of vanilla extract and cinnamon. Pass the mixture through a sieve and blend in diced candied fruit and bits of dark chocolate. Fill the cannoli with the ricotta filling and dip the ends in the crushed pistachio nuts. Sprinkle with very fine icing sugar.

Chef's tips
The cannoli should be filled just before serving: after a few hours they tend to become soft and lose that crispiness which is an essential feature of this delicious dessert.

Cantucci
Cantucci biscuits

Serving 10
Difficulty *Low*
Region *Tuscany*

Sweet

6⅓ oz (180 g) butter – 12⅓ oz (350 g) granulated sugar – 3 eggs – 1 egg yolk – ⅛ oz (4 g) salt – 1 drop (0.25 g) of vanilla – ⅛ oz (4 g) nutmeg, ground – ⅛ oz (4 g) baking powder- 1 lb 1½ oz (500 g) flour – 8¾ oz (250 g) almonds, unskinned.

15 minutes preparation time + 30 minutes cooking time

In a food mixer beat the softened butter with the caster sugar. Add the egg and continue to mix. Add the flour mixed with the baking powder, and then the nutmeg and vanilla. Add the almonds and mix in.

Put the mixture into a pastry bag, and pipe long bars onto a baking tin lined with oven paper, and bake in the oven at 400°F for around 15-20 minutes.

Remove from the oven and allow to cool slightly, then cut the Cantucci by slicing the bars (diagonally) with a smooth-bladed knife to a thickness of about ¼ inch (1 cm). Then put them back into the oven to brown both sides.

Chef's tips
The operation of cutting the strips of dough, once cooked, must be performed swiftly, since otherwise the dough tends to dry up and break during the cutting.

Castagne al cucchiaio
Chestnut and chocolate pudding

Servings 4
Difficulty Medium
Region Abruzzo

Sweet

1 ⅓ lb (600 g) chestnuts – 5 ⅓ oz (150 g) dark chocolate, grated – 4 ¼ oz (120 g) butter – 4 ¼ oz (120 g) sugar – salt.

25 minutes preparation time

Cook the chestnuts in salted water. When cooked, peel and then sieve them. Melt the chocolate in a double boiler, and add it to the warm chestnuts together with the sugar and butter. Stir the mixture well for some time. Line a rectangular mold with parchment paper and grease with butter, spread the mixture on to it, level off and cover with more parchment paper.
Leave in the fridge for at least 4 hours. When it has hardened, cut into shapes (squares, hearts, flowers etc.). Serve with liquid cream.

· *Did you know that…*
Chestnuts were much loved in ancient times. In fact, the Greeks
and the Romans used to transport huge quantities of chestnuts
in their ships, to sell. Chestnuts are the fruit of the chestnut tree,
a long-living tree that originated in Asia Minor, millions of years ago.

Ciambella
Ring cake

Serving 10
Difficulty Low
Region Emilia Romagna

Sweet

2¼ lb (1 kg) all-purpose flour – 14⅛ oz (400 g) sugar – 4 eggs – 1 small sachet of baking powder – zest of 1 lemon, grated – 10½ oz (300 g) butter – milk.

15 minutes preparation time + 25 minutes cooking time

Let butter soften at room temperature before cooking. In a bowl, mix the eggs and the sugar. Add the softened butter, then the lemon zest and, little by little, the flour with the baking powder and lastly the milk. Mix until the mixture is soft and smooth. Grease the mold and put into the oven.
Bake at 400°F (200°C) and after half an hour check if it is cooked. When the "brazadèla" is golden, remove from the oven and leave to cool.

Ciambelline all'anice
Aniseed doughnuts

Servings 4
Difficulty Low
Region Latium

Sweet

14⅛ oz (400 g) flour – ⅓ cup (8 cl) extra virgin olive oil – 3½ oz (100 g) sugar – ⅓ cup (8 cl) white wine – 1 level spoonful of aniseed.

15 minutes preparation time + 10 minutes cooking time

Mix the flour with the sugar, the white wine and the oil. Knead the dough. Add the aniseed. Form the dough into small rolls and make doughnuts by rolling them around a finger. Bake in a moderate oven at 320°F (160°C), until they are golden brown and crunchy.

Ciccitielli
Anise fritters with honey

Serving 10
Difficulty *Low*
Region *Calabria*

Sweet

2¼ lb (1 kg) flour – 7 eggs – 3 egg yolks – 5⅓ oz (150 g) sugar – 5⅓ oz (150 g) lard – 2 liquor glasses of anisette – 10½ oz (300 g) honey – 1 small sachet of baking powder – frying oil – salt.

30 minutes preparation time + 5 minutes cooking time

Break 7 whole eggs, 3 egg yolks into a large bowl, add the sugar, lard, anisette and a pinch of salt. Mix all the ingredients, then slowly sprinkle in the flour bit by bit, mixing continuously until obtaining a very smooth but rather firm mixture.

Lastly, add the baking powder to the dough, cover and leave to rest for an hour. Then roll out the dough with a machine to a thickness of about ⅓ inch (1 cm) thick and cut out various shapes (stars, disks, sticks…). Then deep-fry a few pieces at the time in hot oil, and drain on some straw-paper. Dissolve the honey in half a glass of water and simmer for 10 minutes or so. Pour the honey mixture on the ciccitielli, stirring very gently.

Crema di arance
Orange cream

Servings 4
Difficulty Low
Region Campania

Sweet

2 cups (5 dl) milk – 1½ oz (40 g) starch – 4 egg yolks – 3½ oz (100 g) sugar –
4 oranges – cinnamon.
To decorate: 3½ tablespoons (5 cl) whipping cream – orange zest.
10 minutes preparation time + 15 minutes cooking time

Beat the yolks, sugar, starch and milk with a whisk in a bowl. Bring the milk to the boil over a medium heat and then add to the mixture. Transfer the mixture to a pan and bring to the boil.
When the mixture thickens, remove from the heat and add the juice and grated zest of the oranges.
Cool down the mixture by immersing the pan in a bowl of water and ice. Chill in the fridge.
Serve this delicious Orange Cream, cold, in dessert bowls decorated with a swirl of whipped cream and a piece of candied orange peel, dusted with cinnamon.

Croccante
Almond brittle

Serving 10
Difficulty *Low*
Region *Basilicata*

Sweet

1 lb 1½ oz (500 g) almonds – 1 lb 1½ oz (500 g) sugar – 2 tablespoons (3 cl) water.

10 minutes preparation time + 10 minutes cooking time

Chop the almonds after peeling them. Heat three spoonfuls of water with the sugar and when the sugar has dissolved, add the almonds and stir until they become a deep golden color.
Roll out the boiling paste onto a greased marble surface, cut into lozenges and leave to cool.

Did you know that...
The origins of the almond are to be found in Asia Minor:
as is testified by the wealth of recipes with this most fragrant of nuts.
In antiquity, it was eaten all around the Mediterranean.
In Italy almonds are used to produce true gastronomic pearls,
such as "confetti" (sugared almonds), biscuits, pastries, and marzipan.

Crostata di ricotta romana
Roman ricotta tart

Serving 10
*Difficulty **Medium***
*Region **Latium***

Sweet

For the short crust pastry: 10½ oz (300 g) all-purpose flour – 5⅓ oz (150 g) sugar – 5 ⅓ oz (150 g) butter – 2 egg yolks – 1 whole egg – zest of half a lemon, grated – salt.
For the filling: zest of half a lemon, grated – zest of half an orange, grated – 1 lb 1½ oz (500 g) ricotta cheese, fresh – 8¾ oz (250 g) sugar – 1¾ oz (50 g) chocolate – 2 egg yolks – 1 whole egg – 1 liquor glass of Rum – 1 pinch of cinnamon – 3½ oz (100 g) mixed candied fruit – 1 egg for brushing.

30 minutes preparation time + 20 minutes cooking time

Prepare the short-crust pastry with the flour, butter and eggs, and add a pinch of salt and the grated rind of half a lemon. Leave to rest for 30 minutes wrapped in aluminum foil.
In a bowl, mix the sieved Ricotta, the sugar, two yolks and a whole egg, the grated rind of half a lemon and an orange, a pinch of cinnamon and a small glass of rum, and stir until it becomes a smooth mixture. Roll out part of the short crust pastry and place on the buttered base of a round oven-dish, so that the edges are a little higher than the rim of the oven-dish and pour in the Ricotta mixture in a single even layer. With the remaining dough, prepare some strips to form a circular border around the edge and a grid over the Ricotta.
Brush these strips with the beaten egg and bake in a moderate oven at 350°F (180°C) until the strips are golden and crisp. Allow to cool and before serving dust with vanilla sugar.

Did you know that...
Roman ricotta, is a fundamental ingredient in a number of dishes,
from pasta to desserts. It was already being produced in Roman times
and was mentioned by Cato the Elder.

Dolce di zucca
Pumpkin pudding

Serving 4
Difficulty Medium
Region Piedmont

Sweet

1⅓ lb (600 g) yellow pumpkin – 6⅓ cups (1.5 l) milk – 1¾ oz (50 g) butter – 3½ oz (100 g) all-purpose flour – 2¾ oz (80 g) honey – 2 eggs – 2¾ oz (80 g) sugar.
40 minutes preparation time + 25 minutes cooking time

Put the pumpkin in a glass bowl and cover with plastic wrap. Pierce the plastic wrap and place in a microwave oven for about 20 minutes until the pumpkin is soft enough to mash into a purée.
Meanwhile, melt the butter with the honey diluted in hot water. Add to the casserole with the pureed pumpkin. Stirring constantly, blend in the flour and cook until the mixture thickens. Leave to cool. Add the eggs (only the yolks) and whip the egg whites to stiff peaks.
Gently fold them into the mixture. In a small pan, dissolve the sugar over a low heat and cook until it becomes golden. Pour into a mold. Pour the mixture into the mold coated in caramel and bake in a moderate oven at 350°F (180°C) for 20-25 minutes.
Allow to cool and turn out onto a serving plate.

Dolce freddo ai mirtilli neri
Blueberry tart

Serving 6
Difficulty *Medium*

Sweet

For the short crust pastry: 1 lb 1⅝ oz (500 g) flour – 8¾ oz (250 g) butter – 7 oz (200 g) sugar – 3 eggs – 1 pinch of vanilla powder.
For the filling: 10½ oz (300 g) blueberries – ¾ oz (20 g) sheets of gelatine – 1 lb 1⅝ oz (500 g) ricotta cheese – 7 oz (200 g) whipped cream – 7 oz (200 g) sugar – ⅞ cup (2 dl) white wine, sweet – 1¾ oz (50 g) almonds, peeled – 1 pinch vanilla powder (or vanilla extract) – ⅓ oz (10 g) butter.

30 minutes preparation time + 10 minutes cooking time

To prepare the short crust pastry, mix the softened butter (at room temperature) with the other ingredients to obtain a smooth dough. Cover with plastic wrap and let it rest for a few hours in the fridge. Put the gelatine in cold water and leave to soak. Meanwhile, roll out the short crust pastry with a rolling pin, and use it to line a buttered, circular oven-dish. Trim off the pastry which comes over the rim of the dish, prick the base all over and bake in a preheated oven at 350°F (180°C) for 10-12 minutes.

Blend the sugar and the vanilla into the ricotta and stir until it acquires a smooth creamy consistency, dilute with the whipped cream, and then mix in the blueberries, which have been blanched in the wine. Wring out the gelatine and dissolve it in a double boiler or in a microwave oven, add it to the cream and pour the mixture into the short crust pastry case which by this time will have cooked to a golden brown and cooled down. Put the sweet into the fridge and serve cold sprinkled with sliced almonds.

Fichi al cioccolato
Chocolate coated figs

Serving 4
Difficulty *Low*
Region *Calabria*

Sweet

1 ¾ lb (800 g) dried figs – 5 ⅓ oz (150 g) almonds – 2 cloves – 2 ½ oz (70 g) – candied citron – 1 pinch cinnamon – 3 ½ oz (100 g) dark chocolate, grated – 2 ⅔ oz (75 g) sugar.

20 minutes preparation time + 5 minutes cooking time

Open the the figs and insert the chopped almonds, which have been lightly toasted in the oven, a little of the crushed cloves and some small pieces of the candied citron. Close them firmly with your fingers and put on an oven-tray and bake in the oven.

As soon as they start to brown, remove from the oven and, while they are still hot, roll them in a mixture of grated dark chocolate and sugar. Alternatively, you can even adopt the more common method of dipping the figs, as soon as they come out of the oven, in a casserole with melted chocolate and a little water and a pinch of cinnamon.

The chocolate coated figs should be kept in wooden boxes or in tins lined with wax paper.

Frittelle di mele
Apple fritters

Serving 10
Difficulty Low
Region Trentino
Alto Adige

Sweet

6⅓ oz (180 g) flour – 1 cup (25 cl) milk – 2 eggs – 1 oz (30 g) sugar – 1⅓ tablespoons (2 cl) rum – ¼ oz (6 g) vanilla baking powder – 4 Golden Delicious or Russet apples – oil for frying – icing sugar – 1 pinch of cinnamon (optional) – salt.

20 minutes preparation time + 5 minutes cooking time

Prepare a batter with the milk, flour, eggs, a tablespoon of sugar, a pinch of salt and the rum. To make it lighter, blend in egg whites beaten to stiff peaks or add a bit of vanilla-baking powder.
Peel 3 or 4 large apples (Golden Delicious or Russet), core and cut into slices about ¼ inch (0.5 cm) thick. Immerse the slices in the batter and fry in boiling oil until golden.
Serve hot sprinkled with icing sugar and a pinch of cinnamon to taste.

Frittelle di mele friulane
Apple fritters

Serving 10
Difficulty Low
*Region Friuli
Venezia Giulia*

Sweet

3 ½ oz (100 g) flour – 1 oz (30 g) sugar – 1 tablespoon rum – 1 tablespoon extra virgin olive oil – 2 eggs – 4 apples – juice of 1 lemon – icing sugar.

20 minutes preparation time + 5 minutes cooking time

Put flour, 2 egg yolks, rum, oil and sugar in a bowl and whisk. Add 1 or 2 tablespoons of water to obtain the right consistency. Whip the egg whites into firm peaks and fold into the mixture.
Meanwhile peel the apples, core them, without breaking them and cut them cross-wise into slices about ¼ inch (0.5 cm) thick and marinate them in lemon juice for 5 minutes.
Heat a frying pan full of oil and, one at a time, dry the slices of apple, dip them in the batter and plunge them into the boiling oil and fry on both sides. Drain them on kitchen paper and leave to rest for a few minutes. Sprinkle with icing sugar and serve.
Various types of fruit can be fried in the same way: pears, bananas, apricots, etc.

Frittelle di pane carasau
Sardinian bread fritters

Servings 4
Difficulty Low
Region Sardinia

Sweet

5⅓ oz (150 g) Carasau bread/Sardinian Parchment Bread – 10½ oz (300 g) durum wheat flour – 3 eggs – ½ cup (1 dl) milk – 2¾ tablespoons (4 cl) lukewarm salted water – ¾ oz (20 g) honey.

20 minutes preparation time + 5 minutes cooking time

Mix the flour with the whole eggs, the milk and a little warm salted water. When the dough becomes soft but firm, leave to rest for a few minutes.

Then blend the parchment bread in pieces into the mixture. Make "gnocchi" from the mixture, shaping them with a tablespoon and fry in plenty of boiling oil. Drizzle with honey and serve hot.

Mousse di Parmigiano con pere al vino rosso
Parmesan mousse with pears and red wine

Serving 4
Difficulty *Medium*
Sweet

1 ¼ cups (300g) fresh cream – 7 oz (200g) Parmesan cheese – 1 lb 1 ⅝ oz (500 g) Williams pears – ¼ cup (60 g) dry red wine – ⅓ oz (10 g) sugar – ½ oz (15 g) honey – ½ oz (15 g) gelatine sheet.

2 hours preparation time + 30 minutes cooking time

In a saucepan, bring the cream to a boil. Soften the gelatine in cold water, then squeeze out all the water and add to the cream. Add the grated Parmesan and mix well with a whisk. Chill in the refrigerator for at least 2 hours. Peel and dice the pears. Sauté the pears with the sugar and honey. Add the red wine and reduce until you have a fairly dense syrup.

When the Parmesan mousse has set, transfer it to a pastry bag with a flat tip. Pipe 4 parallel lines of the mousse on each plate and place 2 tbsp of caramelized pears on top. Drizzle with the reduced sauce. Garnish with chives and a Parmesan cheese wafer. You may also serve this dish with hot crostini.

For the Parmesan wafer: put a tablespoonful of grated Parmesan on a sheet of parchment paper and shape it into a circle about one millimeter thick; cook it in a microwave oven for about 20 seconds. Shape it while still hot and then leave to cool.

Panna cotta
Panna cotta

Serving 10
*Difficulty **Medium***
*Region **Piedmont***

Sweet

4 ¼ cups (1 l) fresh cream – ⅞ cup (2 dl) whole milk – 7 oz (200 g) sugar – 4 gelatine sheets – 2 sticks vanilla.

25 minutes preparation time + 10 minutes cooking time

Soak the gelatine sheets in cold water for about 10 minutes. Make a caramel with 3 ½ oz (100 g) of the sugar and coat the inside of one large mold, or several small molds, with it. Pour the cream, the milk and the rest of the sugar into a saucepan and heat over a medium flame and bring almost to the boil, fold in the vanilla and the well wrung out gelatine sheets and stir until the mixture is smooth.

Pour the mixture into the caramel coated mold or molds. Allow to cool and refrigerate for a few hours before serving. To turn out quickly pass the mold over heat, then pour the remaining caramelized sugar over the panna cotta.

Pastiera napoletana
Pastiera (traditional Neapolitan sweet)

Serving 15
Difficulty Medium
Region Campania

Sweet

For the short crust pastry: 10½ oz (300 g) butter – 7 oz (200 g) icing sugar – 4 egg yolks – 1 lb 1⅝ oz (500 g) flour – vanilla.
For the filling: 1 lb 1⅝ oz (500 g) ricotta cheese – 7 oz (200 g) granulated sugar – 7 oz (200 g) soft wheat kernels – ⅓ cup (80 ml) milk – 3 eggs – zest of 1 lemon, grated – 2½ tablespoons (35 ml) orange flower water – vanilla – 2 egg yolks.

30 minutes preparation time + 1 hour and 30 minutes cooking time

Put the flour and butter into a food mixer and mix until they are crumbled. Then blend in the yolks, the icing sugar, the vanilla and continue to mix (being careful not to over-mix). When the dough is ready, wrap it in plastic wrap and leave in the fridge for 2 hours. Roll out the dough to a thickness of ⅛ inch (4 mm). Line the bottom and sides of a cake tin with it and prick the pastry all over with a fork. Put the ricotta into a bowl with the sugar and mix. Then add all the ingredients for the filling, mixing together well, and taking care not to let it collapse. When the filling is finished pour it into the lined cake tin.

Make strips of pastry and lay them crisscross across the top of the pastiera. Bake at 360°F (185°C) for about 1 hour and 30 minutes.

Chef's tips
The filling must be very light, but not too moist. The wheat must be well-cooked. Before removing the pastiera from the tin, wait until it has completely cooled.

Salame di cioccolato
Chocolate salami

Serving 10
Difficulty **Low**
Region **Lombardy**

Sweet

3 ½ oz (100 g) sugar – 3 ½ oz (100 g) butter – 3 ½ oz (100 g) unsweetened cocoa powder – 3 ½ oz (100 g) almonds, or hazelnuts – 7 oz (200 g) dry biscuits – 1 egg.

20 minutes preparation time

Before you begin to make the chocolate salami, remove the butter from the refrigerator and allow it to soften for a few minutes.

Meanwhile, crush the dry biscuits by wrapping them in a napkin and pounding them with a meat-pounder, or with your hands. If you choose to mix the dough with your hands, you should put the butter in a bowl, when it is soft enough, with the rest of the ingredients and begin mixing. If you prefer to use a spoon, start by stirring the butter in a bowl until creamy. Then add the sugar, egg and cocoa, one ingredient at a time. Continue mixing until the mixture is smooth, and then add the cookies and peeled almonds.

Form the mixture into a large salami 2 in (5 cm) wide and wrap it first in plastic wrap, then in aluminum foil. Place in the freezer for at least 30 minutes to harden. Then slice the salami and serve.

Did you know that...
According to historians, Montezuma, the Aztec emperor, drank 40 cups of chocolate a day, always from a different glass.

Sbrisolona
Crumbly cake

Serving 15
Difficulty *Low*
Region *Lombardy*

Sweet

1⅔ lb (750 g) flour – 1⅓ lb (600 g) butter – 1 lb (450 g) icing sugar – 6 eggs – ½ oz (15 g) baking powder – zest of 1 lemon, grated – 1¾ oz (50 g) almonds – 13¼ oz (375 g) finely ground cornmeal.

10 minutes preparation time + 25 minutes cooking time

Put all the ingredients on a work-surface. Mix all the ingredients together to obtain a crumble. Put the mixture into a baking mold.
Lay the unpeeled almonds on top of the crumble mixture. Bake in a preheated oven at 360°F (185°C).

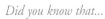

Did you know that...
This is considered to be a Crunch or Crumble; it is a dry sweet that is typical of the Lombardy region. Indeed its name recalls "briciole," the Italian word for crumbs.

Chef's tips
The secret of this sweet lies in crumbling all the ingredients. Do not let the ingredients stick together. The greased cake tin must also be filled by crumbling the mixture into it.

Sorprese alla zucca
Pumpkin surprises

Serving 10
Difficulty *Low*
Region *Emilia Romagna*

Sweet

10½ oz (300 g) pumpkin – 1¾ oz (50 g) sugar – 5 amaretti cookies – 1¾ oz (50 g) raisins – 1 pinch cinnamon powder – 2¾ oz (80 g) mostarda di Cremona (sweet-tart chutney) – 14⅛ oz (400 g) puff pastry (frozen or refrigerated).

1 hour preparation time + 15 minutes cooking time

Bake the pumpkin in the oven at 320°F (160°C) until it is soft. Leave it to cool, then remove the flesh. Mix the pumpkin with the crumbled amaretti cookies, raisins, cinnamon, sugar and diced mostarda.

Roll out the puff pastry until it is less than ½ inch (1 cm) thick and cut it into 2-inch (4-5 cm) squares. Place a tsp of pumpkin mixture in the center of each square and close, giving it the shape you prefer, by either folding the dough, twisting the ends or pinching it.

Place the pastries on a baking sheet lined with parchment paper and bake in the oven at 350°F (180°C) for about 15 minutes.

Remove from the oven and dust with icing sugar, then serve.

Taralli
Taralli

Servings 4
Difficulty **Medium**
Region **Basilicata**

Sweet

4½ lb (2 kg) durum wheat flour – 1½ oz (40 g) fresh yeast – 10 eggs – extra virgin olive oil – 7 oz (200 g) sugar, or 10½ oz (300 g) honey.

30 minutes preparation time + 20 minutes cooking time + 3 hours rising time

Prepare a basic bread dough using the flour, yeast and water.
Let it rise, then add the eggs and the oil necessary to keep the dough soft. Then add the sugar or, if you prefer, the honey. Knead the dough and form the "taralli": rings of dough about 8 inches (20 cm) in diameter.
Leave to rise in a warm place for about 3 hours. "Taralli" can be cooked in two ways: bake on a greased oven tray or by immersing them first in boiling water and then baking in the oven.

Torta a strati con frutta fresca
Fresh fruit layer cake

Servings 4
Difficulty Low

Sweet

3 layers of sponge cake – 4¼ cups (1 l) milk – 3½ oz (100 g) flour – 10½ oz (300 g) sugar – 1 lemon – 1 sachet vanilla powder (or vanilla extract) – 2¼ lb (1 kg) fresh fruit – ½ cup (1 dl) rum – 2⅛ oz (60 g) butter.

16 minutes preparation time + 14 minutes cooking time

Mix 8¾ oz (250 g) sugar, the flour, the vanilla, and the finely grated lemon rind into the milk and heat over a moderate heat until it thickens into a soft cream.

Stir the liquid continuously until it comes to the boil; then, after turning off the heat, blend the butter into the cream and stir again.

Place a layer of sponge cake on a large circular plate, splash it with the rum diluted with an equal amount of water, then pour a third of the cream on top.

Peel and dice the fruit and arrange a third of it on top of the layer of cream. Sprinkle a tablespoon of sugar over the fruit.

Repeat this operation twice. Lastly, put the cake into the fridge for two or three hours to chill.

Torta colonne
Black cherry tart

Servings 4
Difficulty Low
Region Apulia

Sweet

8¾ oz (250 g) sugar – 8¾ oz (250 g) almonds, chopped – 7 oz (200 g) flour – ⅓ oz (10 g) unsweetened cocoa powder – ⅓ oz (10 g) cinnamon powder – 1 sachet vanilla powder (or vanilla extract) – 1 egg + 1 egg yolk – ⅔ tablespoon (1 cl) cherry liqueur – 7 oz (200 g) butter – 7 oz (200 g) black cherry jam.

20 minutes preparation + 40 minutes cooking time

Mix the soft butter with the sugar, the flour, the whole egg, finely chopped almonds, sugar, cocoa, cinnamon, vanilla and cherry liqueur.

Leave the mixture to rest in the refrigerator for an hour.

Roll out ⅔ of the pastry and use it to line a cake pan. Spread the black cherry jam over it, and use the remaining pastry to form strips to place in a grid top of the tart.

Brush the pastry with the egg yolk and bake in the oven at 320°F (160°C) oven for about 40 minutes. Serve cold.

Torta d'Agosto
August cake

Servings 4
Difficulty Low

Sweet

4½ oz (130 g) flour – ½ oz (15 g) baking powder – 4½ oz (130 g) sugar – 2¾ oz (80 g) butter – 1 sachet vanilla powder (or vanilla extract) – 4 white peaches – 3½ oz (100 g) yogurt – 2 tablespoons breadcrumbs, finely ground – 3 eggs – salt.

15 minutes preparation time + 35 minutes cooking time

Mix 2⅛ oz (60 g) of the butter with the sugar in a large bowl and beat until the mixture is smooth and creamy and then add the egg yolks Whisk the egg whites until they form stiff peaks and then fold into the mixture. Mix the flour and baking powder with the vanilla and a pinch of salt and fold in gently, stirring from the bottom to the top until the ingredients are thoroughly blended.
Add the yogurt, peel and dice the peaches and add to the mixture. Pour the mixture into a cake pan greased with butter and sprinkled with breadcrumbs.
Bake in a preheated oven at 350°F (180°C) for 35 minutes.

Torta di nocciole
Hazelnut cake

Servings 4
*Difficulty **Low***
*Region **Piedmont***

Sweet

10½ oz (300 g) hazelnuts – 7 oz (200 g) all-purpose flour – 3½ oz (100 g) melted butter – 5⅓ oz (150 g) sugar – ¼ cup (6 cl) coffee – ⅔ cup (6 cl) milk – 1 sachet baking powder – ⅔ tablespoons (1 cl) extra virgin olive oil – 1⅓ tablespoons (2 cl) rum – 1 pinch vanilla powder.

25 minutes preparation time + 30 minutes cooking time

Lightly roast the shelled hazelnuts on the oven tray, then chop them finely. Mix the chopped hazelnuts with sugar and flour, then blend in three beaten eggs, coffee, milk, oil, rum, vanilla, baking powder, and lastly the melted butter.

Pour mixture into a greased low-edged wide baking pan. The cake should be ¾ inch (2 cm) thick. A good way to do this, is to wrap the mixture completely in aluminum foil, then gently press it with your hands into the mold so that it has a nice even shape.

Bake in a hot oven at 390°F (200°C) for 30 minutes. Dust with icing sugar and serve at room temperature.

Did you know that...
The hazelnut tree, found throughout the whole northern hemisphere, was one of the first fruit trees to be used and cultivated by Man.
The species spread widely and quickly became fundamental for the economy of the first nomadic populations.

Torta di riso
Rice cake

Serving 10
Difficulty Low
Region Emilia-Romagna

Sweet

7 oz (200 g) rice – 3 ½ oz (100 g) sugar – 1 ¾ oz (50 g) candied citron – 1 ¾ oz (50 g) almonds – 3 eggs – 4 ¼ cups (1 l) milk – 2 cups water – 1 ¾ oz (50 g) butter – zest of 1 lemon, grated – pinch of salt – Maraschino liqueur – lemon – ⅓ oz (10 g) butter to grease the oven dish.

30 minutes preparation time + 30 minutes cooking time

Heat the milk over a medium heat in a pan together with the lemon zest and a pinch of salt. When it boils, add the rice and cook until it has absorbed all the liquid. Add the sugar and stir until it dissolves. Leave the mixture to cool. Once the rice is cool, add the eggs, the butter, the candied citron and the almonds. Grease a cake mold and flour it lightly so that the cake comes out more easily. Bake in the oven at 400°F (200°C) for half and hour.
Once it has cooled down and is lukewarm, slice the rice cake into 1 ½ inch (3 cm) side lozenge shapes and brush with the Maraschino liqueur. Serve lukewarm.

Torta Margherita
Margherita cake

Serving 6
Difficulty Low
Region Campania

Sweet

5 ⅓ oz (150 g) flour – 7 oz (200 g) sugar – 1 ¾ oz (50 g) potato starch – 1 ¾ oz (50 g) soft butter – 3 eggs – 7 egg yolks – vanilla – zest of 1 lemon, grated – sprinkling of icing sugar.

30 minutes preparation time + 30 minutes cooking time

Fill a medium sized pan half-full of water and heat. Put a smaller pan, with the butter, in the water in the larger pan. Melt the butter in this bain-marie but do not let it over heat. As soon as it melts, remove from the heat and leave to cool.

Beat the sugar, the eggs and the egg yolks in a bowl with a whisk or electric mixer until the mixture is fluffy. Add the lemon zest and, stirring gently with a spatula, with a circular movement from the bottom to the top, blend in the sieved flower, starch and vanilla. Then add the butter which will have cooled down and, after mixing very gently, pour the mixture into a greased and floured circular cake tin, so that it is ⅔ full.

Bake in the oven at 350°F (180°C) for about 30 minutes.

Zaleti
Cornmeal, pine nut and raisin cookies

Servings 4
Difficulty Medium
Region Veneto

Sweet

12⅓ oz (350 g) cornmeal – 8¾ oz (250 g) all-purpose flour – 1 pinch baking pow-der – 1 pinch vanilla – 5⅓ oz (150 g) butter or lard – 3½ oz (100 g) sugar – 3¼ oz (90 g) raisins – 2½ oz (70 g) pine nuts – 2 eggs – ⅞ cup (2 dl) milk, fresh – grated zest of 1 lemon – sprinkling of icing sugar.

20 minutes preparation time + 20 minutes cooking time

Mix the two kinds of flour with the baking powder and vanilla. Beat the butter with the sugar. Add the raisins, previously soaked in warm water, the pine nuts, eggs, milk and grated lemon zest and mix until you obtain a smooth mixture. Add the sieved flour little by little, stirring continuously to avoid lumps forming.

Shape the mixture into small oval cakes about 3 inches (7-8 cm) long, with your hands. Place them on a parchment paper sheet on an oven tray and bake in a hot oven at 370°F (190°C) for about 20-25 minutes. Leave to cool and then sprinkle with icing sugar.

Did you know that...
These cookies are called zaleti due to their yellow color? "Zaleti" means "little yellow things" in the Veneto dialect.

Coppe d'anguria
Spicy watermelon

Servings 4
Difficulty *Low*

Fruit

½ watermelon – 2 tablespoons (30 g) sugar – 1 pinch vanilla powder (or vanilla extract) – 1 pinch cinnamon – ¼ cup (60 g) gin – 1⅓ tablespoons (20 g) chocolate drops.

15 minutes preparation time

Slice the flesh into large slivers and transfer to four large dessert bowls, with or without a stem, sprinkling the layers with the sugar mixed with the vanilla, and last of all splash with the gin.
Put the filled bowls into the fridge and leave to chill.
Serve well chilled, after sprinkling each portion with chocolate drops and powdered cinnamon.

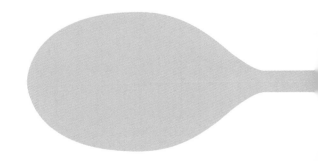

Macedonia d'estate
Summer fruit salad

Serving 10
Difficulty Low

Fruit

2 melons – 3½ oz (100 g) raspberries – Brandy (or "passito" sweet wine).
15 minutes preparation time

Wipe down the outside of the melons with a wet cloth to remove any residual dirt. Cut them in half lengthwise and remove all the seeds using a spoon. Scoop out the flesh of the melon in small balls, using a melon baller, taking care not to damage the skin that should be kept to serve the sweet in. Place the raspberries in a colander and wash carefully for a few seconds, then dry them.
Then place the melon balls and raspberries in a dish and splash with a little brandy or passito. Fill the melon shells with the fruit salad; put them in the refrigerator to chill for half an hour and serve.

Did you know that...
Opinions may vary, but it is likely that melons originated from the tropical
areas of Africa where they are known to have existed before they spread
to the East and subsequently to Europe. Paintings of the fruit found
in the ruins of Pompeii and Ercolano indicate that melons arrived Europe
around the first century BC.

Pesche ripiene con mandorle
Stuffed peaches

Servings 4
Difficulty Low
Region **Emilia Romagna**

Fruit

8 peaches – 4¼ oz (120 g) almonds, peeled – 1 bread roll, soaked in milk – 3 eggs – 5⅓ oz (150 g) sugar.

20 minutes preparation time + 30 minutes cooking time

Choose peaches that are not too ripe. Cut in half, and using a pointed knife, remove the stone and a bit of the flesh, in order to create a space for the filling. Put the peaches in a greased oven dish. Prepare the filling: crush the almonds in a mortar, add the peach flesh, the bread that has been soaked in the milk and wrung out, the egg yolks whisked with the sugar.

Mix together all the ingredients thoroughly and then fold in the egg whites which have been beaten to form stiff peaks. Fill the peaches with the mixture and bake for about 30 minutes at 300°F (150°C). Dust with icing sugar and serve lukewarm.

The almonds can be replaced with chopped macaroons as a variation.

Did you know that...
Originating from China, where they are a symbol of immortality, peaches were brought to the Western world by Alexander the Great.

PIZZA and FOCACCIA

SINCE TIME IMMEMORIAL BREAD, IN ALL ITS PRIMITIVE VARIATIONS OF ROU-
GHLY GROUND CEREALS, COOKED OVER CHARCOAL OR ON HOT STONES, HAS
ALWAYS ACCOMPANIED, IF NOT CONSTITUTED, MAN'S BASIC MEAL.

FOR THIS REASON, THERE IS NO OTHER FOOD THAT HAS SO MANY VARIATIONS AND
DIFFERENT CHARACTERISTICS THAT VARY ACCORDING TO THE REGION, THE CULI-
NARY TRADITION AND THE COUNTRY. INDEED, NOTWITHSTANDING THE SUBSTAN-
TIALLY IDENTICAL METHOD OF PREPARATION, BREAD IS DIFFERENT IN THE VARIOUS
ITALIAN CULTURAL REALITIES (AND ALSO IN OTHER CULTURES WHERE IT IS PART OF
THE STAPLE DIET) AS IT DEPENDS ON THE QUALITY OF THE BASIC ELEMENTS THAT
CHARACTERIZE IT: THE FLOUR, THE WATER, THE RISING PROCESS AND THE SHAPE.
BREAD COMES IN ENDLESS SHAPES; RANGING FROM THE LARGE TRADITIONAL LOA-
VES TYPICAL OF RURAL CULTURE, TO THE SMALLER SHAPES WITH FANCY NAMES
SUCH AS MICHETTE, ROSETTE, SCARPETTE, ... EACH ITALIAN REGION MATCHES THE
VARIOUS TYPES OF BREAD WITH ITS CUISINE AND ITS TYPICAL GASTRONOMIC PRO-
DUCTS; ALL TYPES OF COLD CUTS TO GO WITH SALTED OR EVEN UNSALTED BREAD,
VARIOUS SOUPS, OR AS THEY ARE CALLED IN ITALIAN, "MINESTRE" WITH VEGETA-

BLES AND PULSES WHERE BREAD IS A FUNDAMENTAL INGREDIENT, FISH

SOUP AND BROTHS, FOR WHICH ALL THE COASTAL REGIONS HAVE DIFFE-

RENT VERSIONS AND WHICH ARE ACCOMPANIED BY BREAD TOASTED AND

FLAVORED WITH GARLIC, CHEESE AND VEGETABLES ... BREAD IS ALWAYS PRESENT

EITHER AS A MAIN ITEM OR IN A SUPPORTING ROLE. THERE ARE THEN SPECIAL TY-

PES OF BREAD SUCH AS THE SARDINIAN CARASAU, ALSO KNOWN AS SARDINIAN

PARCHMENT BREAD, PIADINA FROM ROMAGNA AND VARIOUS TYPES OF UNLEAVE-

NED BREAD THAT LOOK LIKE THE ORIGINAL ROMAN AND GREEK TYPES: A SORT OF

THIN DISK STUFFED WITH A HUGE VARIETY OF INGREDIENTS. AND THIS IS WHAT PIZ-

ZA LOOKS LIKE; IT HAS SPREAD FROM THE CAMPANIA REGION TO THE REST OF ITALY

AND INDEED TO THE REST OF THE WORLD, AND FOCACCIA, VERY MUCH THE HERI-

TAGE OF ITALIAN COASTAL REGIONS SUCH AS LIGURIA, CAN NOW BE FOUND

EVERYWHERE. PIZZA IS THE ITALIAN DISH PAR EXCELLENCE. IT OWES ITS ORIGIN AND

GOOD FORTUNE TO NEAPOLITAN CREATIVITY; INDEED TODAY, AS IN THE PAST, THE

BEST PIZZA IS TO BE FOUND IN THE CAPITAL OF THE CAMPANIA REGION: A DISK OF

DOUGH THAT HAS RISEN AND THAT HAS BEEN SPREAD OUT THIN, WITH PEELED TO-

MATOES AND SLICES OF MOZZARELLA OF THE FIORDILATTE TYPE ON TOP (THE BA-

SIC INGREDIENTS FOR ALMOST ALL TYPES OF PIZZA); A GARNISH OF FRESH BASIL LEAVES, COOKED AT A HIGH TEMPERATURE, PREFERABLY IN A TRADITIONAL WOOD-BURNING OVEN, AND BROUGHT OUT OF THE OVEN SOFT AND CRISPY AT THE SAME TIME. WHILE PIZZA WAS ORIGINALLY CONCEIVED AS A "STREET FOOD," AND EVEN TODAY YOU CAN BUY PIZZA FROM STREET VENDORS, OVER THE YEARS IT HAS SPREAD BEYOND ITS ORIGINAL GEOGRAPHIC CONFINES AND, BY ADOPTING VARIATIONS THAT HAVE ENRICHED IT, HAS BECOME SYNONYMOUS WITH THE FOOD OF FRIENDSHIP AND GOOD COMPANY.

FOCACCIA IS A TYPE OF PIZZA WITH A CRISPIER AND OFTEN THICKER DOUGH. IT OFTEN HAS A TOPPING OF VEGETABLES SUCH AS ONIONS, GREEN OR BLACK OLIVES, FRESH OR DRIED TOMATOES, BASIL PESTO, (PROVENÇAL FOCACCIA IS VERY SIMILAR TO THE LIGURIAN TYPE BUT WITH A STRONG CONTRAST IN FLAVORS), BUT IT CAN ALSO HAVE FISH SUCH AS ANCHOVIES, OR CHEESE THAT CAN BE GRATED INTO THE DOUGH TO ADD FLAVOR, OR EVEN ADDED AS A TOPPING; AND IN THE SIMPLEST OF TRADITIONAL CUSTOMS, SMEARED WITH OLIVE OIL AND RUBBED WITH SEA SALT AND HERBS. FOCACCIA IS ESSENTIALLY A SUBSTANTIAL SNACK, RATHER THAN THE ACCOMPANIMENT TO A MEAL.

PIZZA AND FOCACCIA

Calzone
Calzone

Serving 6
Difficulty **Low**
Region **Campania**

Meat

For the dough: 2¼ lb (1 kg) flour – 1 oz (30 g) yeast – 2 tablespoons (3 cl) warm water – 1 oz (30 g) salt – 1 tablespoon granulated sugar – 3 oz extra virgin olive oil – 2⅛ cups (5 dl) water.
For the filling: ⅓ cup (8 cl) extra virgin olive oil – 7 oz (200 g) buffalo-mozzarella cheese – basil leaves – 7 oz (200 g) tomato sauce – 7 oz (200 g) ham.

10 minutes preparation time + 10 minutes cooking time + 60 minutes rising time

Dissolve the yeast in the warm water together with the sugar. On a work-surface make a well in the flour and pour the dissolved yeast into the center of the well. Start kneading and then add the salt. Form an even, smooth, elastic dough. Divide the dough into 6 balls of the same size and leave them to rise.

Once the dough has risen, roll out each ball into a round disk.

Place the tomato sauce in the middle of each disk, the mozzarella cut into regular slices, and the slices of ham.

Fold disk in half and seal the edges, so that the calzone is a half-moon shape.

Spread the tomato sauce over the top of the calzone and place on parchment paper on an over tray, and cook in the oven at 480°F (250°C) until the dough is golden and crispy. Remove from the oven and serve at once.

Chef's Tips
Let the dough rest away from draughts and cover it so that it does not form a crust on the surface.

Erbazzone
Spinach pie

Serving 4
Difficulty Low
Region Emilia
Romagna

Meat

For the filling: 2 lb spinach/Swiss chard boiled and strained – 1¾ oz (50 g) butter – 3½ oz (100 g) lardo (bacon) – 3½ oz (100 g) onion – 1 clove of garlic – 7 oz (200 g) grated Parmesan cheese – 1 oz (30 g) olive oil – salt – pepper.
For the pastry: 5⅓ oz (150 g) flour – 3¼ oz (90 g) lard – ⅛ oz (4 g) salt – 4¾ tablespoons (7 cl) hot water – 1 oz (30 g) bacon or diced bacon fat.

40 minutes preparation time + 25 minutes cooking time

Boil the spinach in salted boiling water. Drain, squeeze out the water and chop up roughly. Over a medium heat, sauté the butter, the chopped lardo and the chopped onion. Add the spinach or Swiss chard with a little of the garlic and cook for five minutes. Leave to cool and then mix in the grated Parmesan, olive oil, pepper and salt.

On a pastry board, mix the flour, lard and hot water to make the pastry. Leave the dough to rest for about 20 minutes and then roll it out with a rolling pin. Line a greased oven-dish with the pastry and spread the filling out on top so that it is about ¾ inch (2 cm) thick. Cover with another slightly larger, puckered sheet of pastry with small pieces of bacon or lard in its folds and bake in a hot oven at 350°F (180°C) until the pastry is golden. Serve while still hot, or warm.

Regional name: Scarpazoun
A classic recipe from Reggio-Emilia.

Chef's Tips
This is a country-style pie,
a traditional snack eaten at picnics
in the country in spring, accompanied
by Lambrusco wine.

Pizza alla romana
Roman-style pizza

Serving 8
*Difficulty **Medium***
*Region **Latium***

Fish

For the dough: 2¼ lb (1 kg) flour – 1 oz (30 g) yeast – 2⅛ cups (5 dl) water, lukewarm – ¾ oz (20 g) salt – ⅓ oz (10 g) sugar.
For the topping: 1 lb 1⅝ oz (500 g) tomatoes – 6 or 7 basil leaves – salt – 40 anchovies – 5½ oz (160 g) desalted capers – extra virgin olive oil.

25 minutes preparation time + 10 minutes cooking time + 1 hour rising time

Dissolve the yeast and the sugar in the water and pour it into the center of a flour well on a work surface. Start kneading, and after a while add the salt. Knead until you have a smooth elastic dough. Set aside for a few minutes, then make 8 small balls. Cover, so they do not dry out on top, and leave to them rise. When the dough has risen to twice its original size, roll out into regular-shaped disks on a floured marble surface.

Make the tomato purée by passing the raw tomatoes through a food mill together with the basil leaves and salt to taste.

Pour out a ladleful of the tomato purée onto each disk of dough. Sprinkle on the diced mozzarella and drizzle over some olive oil. Put 5 anchovies and   oz (20 g) capers on each disk and bake in the oven at 430°F (220°C).

Sfincione
Sicilian-style pizza

Serving 4
Difficulty **Low**
Region **Sicily**

Fish

For the dough: 1 lb 1 ⁵⁄₈ oz (500 g) durum wheat flour – ½ oz (15 g) fresh yeast – ½ oz (15 g) natural sea salt with Italian black olives – 1 cup (2.5 dl) water, lukewarm – 1 ⅓ tablespoons (2 cl) extra virgin olive oil.
For the topping: 1 large onion – 1 ¾ oz (50 g) salted anchovies – 1 oz (30 g) Cacio-cavallo cheese (or goat cheese) – 1 clove of garlic – 1 pinch oregano – salt – 7 oz (200 g) peeled tomatoes – ⅔ tablespoons (1 cl) extra virgin olive oil.

30 minutes preparation time + 20 minutes cooking time + 1 hour rising time

Dissolve the yeast in warm water, make a well in the flour, and add the yeast. Knead the mixture to make a firm smooth dough, and only add the salt some time after mixing in the yeast. When you have finished kneading the dough, cover and leave it rise for an hour.

Tradition has it that by pounding on the dough at the right spot, it makes a particular hollow sound, similar to that of a muted drum.

Make the so called "conza" (the topping) as follows. Slice the large onion and sauté in extra-virgin olive oil over a low flame. Add the peeled tomatoes and the clove of garlic. Cook until it becomes a thick fragrant sauce, and remove the garlic. Spread the dough out with your hands in a greased baking tin to a thickness of about ¾ inch (2 cm).

Press bits of the desalinated and filleted anchovies into the dough and place thin slices of Caciocavallo cheese on top. Top with a generous layer of sauce and sprinkle with grated Caciocavallo cheese and fresh oregano. Drizzle with olive oil and put into a very hot oven at 430°F (220°C).

If the sauce is not sufficiently dense, you can add some breadcrumbs, that have been toasted in a little olive oil in a frying pan, to the grated Caciocavallo cheese.

Calzone barese
Calzone Bari-style

Serving 6
Difficulty *Medium*
Region *Apulia*

Vegetable

For the dough: 1 lb 1⅝ oz (500 g) flour – ⅞ oz (25 g) fresh yeast – ⅝ cup (1.5 dl) water – ½ cup (1 dl) extra virgin olive oil.
For the filling: 14⅛ oz (400 g) tomatoes, ripe – 5⅓ oz (150 g) salted ricotta – 3½ oz (100 g) black olives – 1 onion – 3½ tablespoons (5 cl) extra virgin olive oil – salt – pepper.

10 minutes preparation time + 20 minutes cooking time + 60 minutes rising time

Pour flour onto a pastry board and mix in the yeast dissolved in a little warm water, a pinch of salt and a generous half glass of oil. Knead dough until soft and flexible, then cover with a cloth and let it rise for about an hour. In a saucepan, soften a sliced onion in the oil, and then add peeled, chopped tomatoes.

Reduce the sauce for a few minutes, then season with salt and pepper, and add pitted chopped olives. Remove from the heat and blend in the sieved salted Ricotta cheese, and mix well. Roll out the dough into two sheets, one larger than the other. Using the larger sheet, line an oiled pan, then spread the sauce over it and cover with the second sheet, carefully folding the edges together. The calzone must be baked in a very hot oven at 475°F (240°C) for about twenty minutes.

During Lent, a few salted filleted anchovies are finely chopped and added to the sauce together with the olives.

Did you know that…
Calzone is a delicious variation of the Italian bread making tradition
that is found throughout the peninsula, in all regions, together
with pizzas and focacce with typical local products used for the filling.
Originating in Apulia, it is prepared using the same dough
as for pizza and it also has a different filling

Focaccia
Focaccia

Serving 4
Difficulty Low
Region Liguria

2¼ lb (1 kg) flour, white – 1 oz (30 g) fresh yeast – 2⅛ cups (5 dl) water – ⅞ cup (2 dl) extra virgin olive oil – 1 oz (30 g) salt – pepper.
Basting solution: 3½ tablespoons (5 cl) water – 2 tablespoons (3 cl) extra virgin olive oil – pinch (2 g) of salt.

10 minutes preparation time + 20 minutes cooking time + 100 minutes rising time

Mix the flour and the yeast with the water and add the salt at the end in order to avoid burning out the yeast. Let it rise for at least three hours covered with a cloth.
Roll out the dough so that it is a uniform thickness of about ¾ inch (2 cm) and place in a slightly oiled rectangular baking tin. Make some small dimples by pressing down with your fingers randomly. Let the dough rise for at least another 40 minutes. Mix the basting solution and cover the focaccia with it. Bake in a hot oven at 400°F (200°C) for about twenty minutes.

Regional name: Fûgassa

Focaccia alle cipolle
Focaccia with onions

Serving 4
Difficulty Low
Region Apulia

Vegetable

For the dough: 2¼ lb (1 kg) flour – 1 oz (30 g) salt – 2½ tablespoons (35 ml) extra virgin olive oil – ½ oz (15 g) granulated sugar – 1 oz (30 g) yeast – 2⅛ cups (5 dl) water.

For the filling: 8¾ oz (250 g) onion – 3½ tablespoons (5 cl) extra virgin olive oil – 1 oz (30 g) ricotta forte cheese – 1¾ oz (50 g) cherry tomatoes – 1¾ oz (50 g) black olives – ¾ oz (20 g) grated Pecorino cheese – salt – pepper.

30 minutes preparation time + 30 minutes cooking time + 100 minutes rising time

Mix the flour with the yeast, the water and add the salt at the end so that it does not inhibit the growth of the yeast. Cover with a cloth and leave the dough to rise for at least an hour. Chop the onion à la julienne and sauté in the oil in a pan over a medium heat. Add the pitted black olives, ricotta forte and plum tomatoes and cook for a few minutes. Remove from the heat, add the Pecorino cheese, season with salt and pepper and let it cool.

Roll out half of the dough and line a greased baking tin with high sides. Spread the filling evenly over the dough and cover with the remaining dough. Seal the edges well so that the filling does not leak out. Sprinkle oil over the surface of the focaccia and decorate the edges of the focaccia with the help of a fork. Prick the surface all over so that air bubbles do not form inside while baking. Leave to rise for 40 minutes and bake in the oven at 390°F (200°C) until the focaccia is golden and crispy.

Serve hot, wait a few minutes before cutting into squares.

Focaccia ligure alle erbe aromatiche
Ligurian focaccia with herbs

Serving 4
Difficulty *Low*
Region *Liguria*

Vegetable

2¼ lb (1 kg) flour – 1 oz (30 g) fresh yeast – ⅝ cup (1.5 dl) extra virgin olive oil – 2 cups (450 ml) water – ⅞ oz (25 g) fine salt – ⅓ oz (10 g) coarse salt – ¼ oz (7 g) sage – ¼ oz (7 g) rosemary – ⅛ oz (4 g) thyme.

30 minutes preparation time + 20 minutes cooking time + 100 minutes rising time

Mix the flour and the yeast with water, the chopped herbs and the oil, and add the salt at the end in order to avoid inhibiting the growth of the yeast. Cover with a cloth and leave to rise for at least one hour.

Grease a baking tray and stretch out the dough in it using your hands. Brush the top of the dough with oil; sprinkle with coarse salt and let it rise for a further 40 minutes.

Bake in a hot oven at 390°F (200°C) until the top is crispy.

Chef's Tips
To give the right color to the focaccia, add a teaspoon of sugar to the dough.

Piadina
Piadina

Serving 8
Difficulty *Low*
Region **Emilia Romagna**

Vegetable

2¼ lb (1 kg) flour - ¾ oz (20 g) salt – 1 oz (30 g) bicarbonate of soda – 7 oz (200 g) melted lard (or olive oil) – 1½ cups (35 cl milk) - ¾ cup (15 cl) lukewarm water.

30 minutes preparation time + 25 minutes cooking time

Pour the flour out on a pastry board and form a well. Dissolve the baking soda in the milk at room temperature. Mix it into the flour, together with the other ingredients.

Knead the dough well with your hands until you have a smooth, firm dough. Divide the dough into 8 balls (called "panett" in the local dialect), cover with a kitchen cloth and leave to rise for about 30 minutes. Then, the balls should be kneaded briefly and rolled out with a rolling pin to obtain disks of about 6 inches (15 cm) in diameter and ¹⁄₁₀ inch (3 mm) inch thick.

Place a flat baking tray on the stove-top. When hot, put a disk of dough on top.

Keep an eye on the piadina while cooking, using a fork to prod the dough so that air bubbles do not form. The piadina must be prodded all over to avoid large bubbles forming so that the piadina remains flat and has its characteristic light and dark spots on the surface.

Did you know that…
Filled with local culinary specialties and sold in the food stalls along the coast, the piadina is without a doubt the most famous food from Romagna. Already known and prepared back in the 16th century when it was considered to be a bread-substitute eaten between one weekly batch of bread and another.

Chef's Tips
A piadina is typically filled with cheese and/or cold-cuts.

Pizza Margherita
Pizza Margherita

Serving 8
Difficulty Medium
Region Campania
Vegetable

For the dough: 2¼ lb (1 kg) flour – 1 oz (30 g) yeast – 2⅛ cups (500 ml) water, lukewarm – ⅓ oz (10 g) sugar – ⅓ oz (10 g) salt.
For the topping: ⅓ cup (8 cl) extra virgin olive oil – 1¾ lb (800 g) buffalo-mozzarella cheese – 40 basil leaves – 14⅛ oz (400 g) fresh tomatoes – salt.

30 minutes preparation time + 20 minutes cooking time + 100 minutes rising time

Dissolve the yeast and the sugar in a little water, empty the flour onto a work surface and make a well in it, then pour the dissolved yeast into the center of the flour well. Start kneading, and after a while, add the salt. Knead until you have a smooth elastic dough. Set aside for a few minutes, then make 8 small balls, cover so that the top part does not dry out, and leave them to rise.

When the dough has risen to twice its original size, roll out the balls of dough into regular-shaped disks on a floured marble surface.

Make tomato puree by passing the peeled tomatoes through a food mill and pour out a ladleful of the tomato purée onto each disk of dough. Sprinkle diced mozzarella over the disks and drizzle with oil. Arrange basil leaves over the surface so that they are slightly covered with tomato puree; to avoid them being burned. Put the pizzas in the oven at 430°F (220°C).

Remove from oven when the edges of the pizza are golden and crispy.

Did you know that…
It is said that this pizza was created by Raffaele Esposito in 1889 in honor of Queen Margherita of Savoy, *to bear witness to the affection of the people of Naples who saw her, as the young bride of Umberto I, ascend the throne in their own city.*

Chef's Tips
The Neapolitan pizza has three fundamental features: soft dough, a crisp edge and the topping.

Pizza rustica
Rustic pizza

Serving 4
Difficulty **Medium**
Region **Apulia**

Vegetable

For the dough: 1 lb 1⅝ oz (500 g) flour – 2 potatoes, medium sized – 1 cup (2.5 dl) water, lukewarm – ½ oz (12 g) fresh yeast (half a cube) – 1 pinch sugar – ⅓ oz (10 g) salt.
For the filling: 4 medium onions, thinly sliced – 30 black olives, pitted – ⅓ oz (10 g) capers – 4 "San Marzano" tomatoes, ripe – ½ cup (1 dl) extra virgin olive oil.

30 minutes preparation time + 40 minutes cooking time + 2 hours rising time

Boil the potatoes, peel when still hot and mash them in a bowl. Blend in the flour together with the yeast, that has been dissolved in warm water, to make a firm dough, and then add a pinch of salt, a pinch of sugar and a tablespoon of oil; cover and leave to rise for at least a couple of hours in a warm room. Boil the onions in a little water for about 10 minutes and strain. Heat 2 tablespoons (3 cl) of oil over a low heat and when it is hot sauté the onions but do not let them turn brown. At this stage, add the capers and chopped tomatoes, mix well and cook for 10-15 minutes. Add salt to taste, remove from the heat and add the olives sliced into rounds.
Divide the dough into two equal parts and spread one part into an oiled baking tin. Spread the filling over the dough and cover with the remaining dough. Brush the top with a little oil and bake in a hot oven at 350°F (180°C) for about 30 minutes.

Did you know that…
In ancient Rome, street vendors used to sell flat-bread that can be considered the forerunner of modern pizza.
The first signs of the existence of the word "pizza" date back to 997 in the Vulgar Latin of Gaeta, but it was only in the 16th century in Naples that it came to be associated with flat-bread.

MICHAEL WHITE

Executive Chef and Partner, Alto, Convivio and Marea

ALTHOUGH MICHAEL WHITE'S SOULFUL, FLAVORFUL INTERPRETATIONS OF ITALIAN CUISINE INDICATE OTHERWISE, HE IS NOT AN ITALIAN NATIVE WHO ABSORBED GENERATIONS OF RECIPES AT BIRTH. HE IS, IN FACT, A MIDWESTERNER WHO SPENT THE MAJORITY OF HIS CHILDHOOD DAYS IN BELOIT, WISCONSIN PLAYING FOOTBALL AND SWIMMING COMPETITIVELY. AT THE TIME, COOKING WAS SIMPLY AN ENJOYABLE FAMILY PASTIME. BY WHIM OR INTUITION, WHITE DECIDED TO TRY HIS HAND AT CULINARY SCHOOL, PURSUING A CAREER OUT OF SOMETHING THAT HAD BEEN ONLY A PASSING FANCY. HE ENROLLED AT KENDALL CULINARY INSTITUTE IN 1989 AND JUST A YEAR LATER, SECURED A POSITION PREPPING IN CHICAGO'S MOST FAMOUS ITALIAN RESTAURANT, SPIAGGIA. HE SPENT A YEAR AND A HALF LEARNING FROM CHEF PAUL BARTOLOTTA AND, WANTING TO FIND THE ORIGIN OF HIS MENTOR'S AWE-INSPIRING RECIPES, HE FOLLOWED THE CHEF'S FOOTSTEPS TO ITALY.

HE TRAINED WITH THE VENERATED ITALIAN CHEF VALENTINO MARCATTILII AT RISTORANTE SAN DOMENICO IN IMOLA AND IT WAS THERE, THAT HE BEGAN HIS ITALIAN TRANSFORMATION. WHITE RETURNED TO THE US IN 2001 WITH HIS TECHNIQUE FIRMLY ROOTED IN HIS PROFOUND RESPECT FOR ITALY'S CULINARY TRADITIONS AND A HIGH-SPIRITED DESIRE TO SHOWCASE THE COUNTRY'S FINEST INGREDIENTS AND MOST REVERED RECIPES. HE RETURNED TO SPIAGGIA AS CHEF DE CUISINE AND IN 2002, HE TOOK NEW YORK BY STORM AS EXECUTIVE CHEF OF FIAMMA OSTERIA. IN 2007, WHITE PARTNERED WITH NEW YORK'S ACCOMPLISHED RESTAURATEUR CHRIS CANNON AND TOOK THE HELM OF THE JAMES BEARD AWARD WINNING (2003) L'IMPERO AND ALTO. IN MAY 2009, THE TWO OPENED MAREA, A RESTAURANT DEVOTED TO THE BOUNTY OF THE SEA.

ENDLESSLY INSPIRED BY THE NOTION OF TASTE MEMORY, WHITE STRIVES TO RECREATE THE SENSORY FEEL OF TRUE ITALIAN DINING EXPERIENCES WITH EACH DISH HE CREATES.

RECIPE INDEX

PHOTO CREDITS

All photographs are by ACADEMIA BARILLA except the following:
page 5 and cover Andrew Unangst/Getty Images
page 341 Chris Bayley/Photolibrary Group

INGREDIENTS INDEX

MY FAVORITE RECIPES

505

511

515